I0143551

MORE *from the* MASTER

JACK RINELLA

M○RE *from the* MASTER

JACK RINELLA

With an Introduction by
Chuck Renslow

Rinella Editorial Services

Copyright © 2008 by Jack Rinella

All rights reserved. No part of this book may be reproduced or transmitted in any form or by any means, electronic or mechanical, including photocopying, recording, or by any informational storage or retrieval system, except with permission in writing from the publisher.

Published by
Rinella Editorial Services
4205 North Avers Avenue
Chicago, IL 60618 USA

www.RinellaEditorial.com

Book and Cover designs
by
Michael Tallgrass

Contact him at mtallgrass@comcast.net

Library of Congress Control Number: 2008908539

ISBN 0-940267-12-8
ISBN 978-0-940267-12-1
Printed in the United States of America

Distributed by SCB Distributors

Dedicated to You

My Reader

Who has empowered me to be myself.

I hope my writing does the same for you.

Other Titles by Jack Rinella

The Master's Manual

The Compleat slave

Partners in Power

The Toy Bag Guide to Clips and Clamps

Becoming a Slave

Philosophy in the Dungeon

The Dictionary of Scene-Friendly Terms

Table of Contents

Introduction
by
Chuck Renslow

How appropriate to have been asked to write this forward for Jack Rinella's book, *More from the Master*. Like many of his readers, I first became acquainted with Jack through his writings. In 1992, Jack's "Leather Views" column began appearing in Gay Chicago Magazine. I was intrigued by his subject matter and mystified that we didn't already know each other, given that we lived in the same city and moved in the same circles. I remember asking several people whether or not they knew this Jack Rinella. They did not.

I continued reading Jack's work, week after week and finally came to the conclusion that I ought to know him so I took the initiative of sending him a little note about something he'd written. Along with that note, I invited him to join me and my family for dinner.

Since then, Jack has been back to our house so many times that I couldn't guess the number. Sometimes for dinner, sometimes for parties and holidays, sometimes for meetings, and sometimes just to talk. Jack has become a true friend. I've enjoyed his counsel and he mine.

The point is, like most of you, I came to know Jack Rinella through his written words. By the time I asked him to dinner and had the good fortune of meeting him face to face, I already knew who he was. I'd read his thoughts. I'd been inside his mind.

Jack was writing about one of my favorite subjects, what we used to call "rough sex" and now call "Leather." I followed him the way one master follows another, sizing him up. I read what he wrote and took it in and analyzed it to see if it made sense to me. Eventually, whether or not I agreed with him, I incorporated what Jack had written into my own understanding of my community and my self. I wrote and rewrote my own 'leather views' in my mind. I bonded with Jack Rinella there, in my mind. Here in this newest collection of his weekly columns, you'll do the same.

More from the Master, as Jack Rinella writes it, is a collection of essays on SM and its practice as a lifestyle. It will not engage everyone, but for those who live in or aspire to live in that lifestyle these columns are invaluable insights into Jack's lifetime of experiences. Beyond being a writer, in writing "Leather Views," Jack has become a teacher.

Jack's columns didn't always tell me something new, though they often offered a new perspective. I have enjoyed Jack's friendship over the years, but first I enjoyed his writing. I know you will too.

Chuck Renslow

Introductions

Taking a Risk Is What It Takes

February, 2004[1]

A reader once asked about Novice Night, a monthly get-together I hosted in the early 90's, and ended the conversation with the idea that he didn't know if he would attend because "I don't know anyone there."

Well, meeting people is one of the reasons that activities like Novice Night are held. It seems pretty reasonable to me that if you want to meet people you go to places where you can meet people. Not to do so becomes a circular argument and a self-fulfilling prophecy: "I don't know anyone so I don't go places where I will meet someone and therefore I never meet anyone and hence I don't know anyone."

There's nothing wrong with being alone, but if you're lonely, you probably have no one but yourself to blame. This column may sound more like Ann Landers than leather, but as I've written before, everything in the leather scene involves human beings and thus those same interpersonal skills so necessary at work, at school, at home, etc. apply just as importantly in a dungeon or a leather bar.

In fact, the only way to get involved in leather is to become friends with leather folk, play with them, learn from them, be with them, and become one of them. Of course, to do any of this you have to meet at least one of them. That naturally leads to the number one question, "How do I meet people into leather?"

In non-leather situations, the same question is just as popular. "How do I meet someone?" The answer is simple. You've got to take a risk.

Fear holds us back from risk-taking. For some of us that may mean just a bit of hesitancy, a pause before we plunge. Others, though, are caught in a paralysis of inactivity, a few to the sad point where they are rendered helpless. The rest of us fall into some spot on the wide spectrum between doubt and action.

My friends always think I'm joking when I say I'm a shy person who pretends to be an extrovert. Few of them know me

---

1 The dates reflect the original composition of the essays, though the essays have been edited occasionally for clarity and correction.

well enough to understand that I too have my doubt, my confusion, and my fear. But I also have the desire to move on, to get over fear and doubt, to resolve whatever issue or dilemma confronts me. If I don't like where I'm at, I do my best to change. My best may not be an immediate remedy, but I know that eventually I'll get to where I want to be.

It's not always as easy as I'd like. After all, everything has a degree of risk associated with it. Risk is pandemic to life on this planet.

Certain forces would have us believe that risk can be eradicated, or that to take risks is unwise, or that the worst always happens so we must not disturb the comfortable status quo. The nay-sayers have their point: inactivity is always easier. Inertia is on the side of doing nothing. The known, unpleasant as it may be, is always a little less frightening than its alternative.

But, shy as I am (grin), I'm still a risk taker. I'm not sure why that is so, but I am. Perhaps it's genetics (male, Caucasian, Southern Italian), upbringing (son of immigrant offspring, entrepreneurial parents), environment (America in the second half of the twentieth century), or the stars (OK, I'm a Sagittarian)! I do take risks. Sometimes they may seem crazy but in a closer analysis, at least as I analyze them, they don't seem all that risky.

I got to the point of being able to take risk by not doing so. After years of "living by the book," at least in most ways (grin, again), I found myself nearing bankruptcy, at odds with my children, totally and continually depressed, fighting with my lover, and broke. Being broke, of course, may be the strongest motivator. If you don't have two cents to rub together, believe me, you'll find a solution to change the situation really quick.

In those days, I found myself crying myself to sleep, wondering what misfortune would happen next. I felt -- and to be honest it was really only feelings, not "reality" --- that life was the pits, that I was a real fuck-up, and that I had nothing to lose. And so I decided to take a risk.

Well, as most of you know, everything came out right. As bad as things might have been, that's how good they are now. It proves to me that taking risks is what it takes. So here I am writing about risk-taking because I see that as the only way to get from here to there, to find the friend, the job, the experience, the money, the love, the situation that you seek.

The hard, cold truth is that nothing is without risk. No matter what course of action you take, even the course of no action, you run the risk of making things worse, missing your mark, or just living in that same old rut.

But the truth of the matter is that we most often over-estimate the consequences of our actions. The reality is that nothing is ever as important as we think, that the worst never happens, and that in the grand scheme of things we can only see darkly, as if through a lens (rose-colored sometimes, but too often it's really a charcoal, foggy, gray.)

So take that risk with the following guidelines:

▶ The worst never happens. Think of what the worst might be and chances are that your fears are not only ungrounded, but that the result will fall far short of the disaster you expect. After all, you won't become a laughing stock, you won't really lose everything, and most people won't even notice.

▶ Nothing ventured, nothing gained. OK, I admit that I've bought into many (but not all) of my mother's clichés. Clichés are clichés because of their veracity. If you don't venture, you won't achieve your goal. If your lifestyle maintains the status quo, guess what you'll get. Put differently, if you always do what you've always done, you'll always get what you've always gotten.

▶ By all means, hedge your bets. The reason I can take as many chances as I do is that I always leave myself a way out. I don't go whole hog, just hog enough to see what happens. For instance, I think I'm going to win the lottery --- now there's risk taking for you --- but do I buy a thousand dollars' worth of tickets, sell my car to place a bet, or take money meant for rent to the lottery man? No, I involve myself instead in a few dollars a week that I can afford and remember that I may not win the lottery this week so I'd better live like I won't win it this week, but play like I will.

▶ Take the risks in easy steps. Joe, for instance, is thinking about moving to another city to become someone's slave. That is a big risk, but since he is unemployed, not as big as if he had to quit a job to do so. The idea overwhelms him, though being someone's slave is all he ever thinks about. How shall he handle it? Take your risks in easy doses, Joe. Don't move to the other city forever, just commit yourself to one week. Take a smaller risk first and see what happens.

Likewise that reader who didn't know anyone at Novice Night (not true because he had met me!) doesn't need to go to Novice Night as if he were the facilitator or the nation's most knowledgeable leather person. Rather all he has to do is show up and stand by the door.

If we all have blood on our jackets, machetes in our hands, and there are nooses ready to string him up, he can run home quickly without even taking his jacket off. After all, that is the worst that can happen, isn't it?

Well, maybe his mother will be there too, but I doubt it. The truth of the matter is that by showing up, he risks only the price of a round trip taxi cab and a few hours' boredom.

So weigh the risk. I'm not sure what the cab will cost each way, but the boredom will be bearable, at least as bearable as being home alone for the twentieth night in a row. Simply put, if the gains outweigh the risk's cost, go for the gain and ignore the cost. You have nothing to lose but the status quo.

Enough talk. Here's to it and to it, and to it again. And if **5** you don't do it when you first get to it, you may never get to it to do it again. Take a chance on having a great week.

Take It Slow and Easy

June 20, 1999

Three questions all get the same answer, printed in the title of this column. One was from a guy who wanted to know:

"My fiancé is turned on by bondage and has introduced me to this new topic. He asked me to read your web page on introductory bondage. (I found this to be very well written and very informative for a person who already knows that they are turned on by bondage.) I am from a rural area in the Midwest and have had no exposure to bondage prior to meeting my fiancé. Do you have any helpful hints to introduce bondage to a very non-experienced person? This is new to us, new for him because his previous girlfriend was the one who had experience and new to me completely because believe it or not, bondage has not reached the whole USA yet. I appreciate your taking the time to read this. If you have any helpful ideas I would (and I know my fiancé would too) appreciate hearing them."

And another one writes:

"What about ball gags? My wife is experimental but has not done anything like this before. I want to gag her for the sexy look. I am a fireman and am very good with my knots and she enjoys the process of me tying her up because I stop periodically to ask her how she is, then we have sex. I bought a ball gag but it is too big. She has a gag reflex (except during a blowjob). What else can I use? Please help."

The third question came from a guy who lives "400 miles from Los Angeles" and wants to go to L.A. to meet a Master to be the guy's slave. Seems they've never met. It also turns out that the guy has never had sex with a man before and is fearful, to say the least.

Some 24 or so years after my first experience of SM, it's easy to forget that I was once in the same situation. I get the idea that many of my readers never figure out that once upon a time, even if it was a long time ago, I was new to all this Leather stuff.

Mom says "There's a first time for everything." Even if now I smile and say "Been there, done that," there was a time when I hadn't done anything like that at all.

The simple fact is that we get from entry-level, no-experience-at-all status to being a jaded know-it-all only one step at a time. It's best that all of those steps be small steps. In many cases we have no choice but to do it that way.

Oh, I've met a number of guys who have taken to Leather "whole hog," but even then it was because they happened to have met the right people at the right time. Often, too, those who plunge in quickly find it necessary to back away for a time to figure things out.

Kink can be overwhelming. In order not to be overwhelmed one must take it slowly and, as Patrick adds, "Take lots of deep breaths."

So to answer my friends, I'll start out by saying to simply buy a shank of rope, either cotton or nylon, and cut it into lengths of three to six feet. If it's nylon, you can use the flame of a candle to carefully melt the ends so they don't unravel. I use rubber cement to do the same with cotton rope, soaking the ends and letting them dry on a piece of wax paper.

As to a gag, you might just want to go back to the store and buy a smaller one, but really there are lots of other things that work: lingerie, jock straps, socks, rope, and leather thongs come to mind immediately.

You could also get a dowel about an inch in diameter and six inches long. Make sure it is clean and smooth. Attach a length of leather to each end and it makes a nice bridle-like gag. You could take it one step further and add two lengths of leather at each end, one short to tie around the back of the head, the other long enough to use as reins.

With this gizmo you can play horsy... riding your bottom or fucking him or her while you pull on the reins. You see, none of this is really very complicated. As the second reader noted, "I stop periodically to ask her how she is, then we have sex." Taking it slowly and checking to make sure that everything is OK is really the essence of being safe. What do you look for? Check to make sure that hands and feet are warm and that there is no sign that they are "falling asleep" or becoming numb.

And for my third reader, I would advise him to get a little experience before he tries to get a lot of experience. Have a little bit of sex before you have lots of sex. Explore closer to home where you know your way around, where you have friends to help you through the experience and to process the feedback later.

OK, so you're in "no sex land." I will protest that it makes no difference at all. After all, I got my experiences in Ft. Wayne, Indiana. That's not exactly known as the Gay Leather Capital of the Universe.

How to do this? Cruise locally. Go to nearby bars. Use chat rooms filled with people from your city. Answer ads in local newspapers. Even if you are in Podunk, you can plan an excursion for a night or two to a nearby larger city. Get a copy of a Gay travel guide. Even if you're straight, a bartender in a Gay bar can tell you where to find information about heterosexual groups.

Afraid of a Gay bar? Try magazines, especially the Leather Journal (http://www.theleatherjournal.com) to find the names and addresses of local clubs and groups. Believe me when I say the club scene is a great way to learn. And I assure you it's very discreet.

You may have to wait some time for a club to answer your letter or phone call. After all, they're volunteers. They'll ask a few questions and will want to meet you before you get an invite to a meeting, but you'll find them helpful and welcoming.

This whole process has three steps, really: Get to know someone. Once you know them, you'll be able to trust them. Once you trust them, you'll be able to make some kind of commitment. You can't do any of that without the "getting to know you," or in the case of Leather, the getting to know it, stage. Learn by easy, slow, and relaxed steps. There's no need to hurry. Leather is a wide wonderful world and it's waiting for you, even if you take your own sweet time getting there.

Swimming and Other Examples

December 29, 2006

My dubious distinction as a writer generates a great number of inquiries from folks who are seeking entry into our subculture. They range from "Where can I get a book" to "I want to serve you in the darkness of your dungeon forever." Now don't think that I call the distinction "dubious" because I doubt my writing abilities. It's dubious because my imagined stature keeps many of these newbies from actually venturing into my dungeon. As I wrote recently, "It's no fun being on a pedestal all by yourself." Unfortunately every time I try to jump off, most people just think "That's Jack" and put me back up on it. Oh well, none of that has anything to do with this week's topic, which I call swimming.

It doesn't have to be about swimming. It could be about bicycling or scuba diving or brain surgery, for that matter. I really want to write about the process of entry into our subculture and progression to the place of expert. You see, if there are more people entering, there's more fresh meat for me. Likewise, if more people become experts, I won't be the only one on the pedestal, though to be honest I have yet to be able to play with any of my heroes, and I hope J. B. is reading this! Honestly, though, I did play with Jason and he's played with John Preston, so I guess that counts for something.

Let me state the two reasons why this topic is important, besides the crass attempt to improve my sex life. First it serves as a guide to those newbies afraid, so to speak, of the water. Secondly, everyone else (that's you, devoted long-time reader) needs to know how to help those newbies join us. There are many ways to learn how to swim and the example of swimming, like sky-diving or diamond cutting, serves as an apt description of the process. You know, some people don't swim because they are afraid of the water, or afraid of the sharks, or don't know where the water is safe for swimming, i.e., free of contaminates. Can you relate? You know, some people don't play with us because they are afraid of what they'll find out about themselves, or afraid of the abusers (they think are) among us, or don't know where to find a group of safe, sane, and consensual adults.

Some swimming instructors (poor ones at that) think that throwing a person into water over his or her head is the way to teach someone to swim. Others understand that it's better to begin more slowly. Some use safety devices such as a buoyancy jacket or an inner tube. To advance to more skilled swimming, smart learners use swim coaches, practice extensively, watch videos and sporting events, build other necessary skills, do research on the topic by reading books and attending lectures on the topic, etc.

You see, newbies need to avail themselves of an educational process and we need to be able to understand and facilitate that process. Most importantly we have to let them know that there is a process to getting to know us, getting to know all about us. Unfortunately there is a strong erroneous mystique about what it is that we do. Namely that we kinksters enter into the subculture with full-blown expertise and that we expect others to do so as well.

Of course, I am exaggerating here. There are many organizations that give good introductory seminars, that have welcoming committees, that help newbies get their "feet wet" without getting in "over their heads." On the other hand, spend some time counting and you'll see that too often we share the attitude that a newcomer ought to "jump right in."

I understand the feelings. I have a date with a newbie tonight. I've planned to let him get to know me conversationally, then we'll go out to Anna Maria's Pasteria (my favorite restaurant), where I'll use his stomach to get to his heart, and then we'll come back to my place and we'll play. My fantasy life hopes that I can collar him then and there, make him sign a life-long contract, and he'll move right in to be my sex slave and domestic servant forever.

We are, after all, a subculture that thrives on fantasy and I've got lots of them to keep my libido hot and strong for a long, long time. But fantasy is only the lure into our midst and it cannot ever be, and must not be, more than that. We cannot base our welcoming or our educating on fantasy. Too often, of course, we do.

Can you imagine if brain surgeons acted that way? Let's see. A nineteen year-old watches *Leave It to Beaver* and decides to become a brain surgeon just like Ward Cleaver. (I don't know what Ward did for a living, but I thought he was a brain surgeon.) So he goes to the brain surgeon club, buys the right clothing, complete with cap and mask. He buys a regulation satchel and stops at the brain surgeon sales table in the vendor area of the hospital to buy sounds, needles, thread, knives, and a cute little hammer to hit people on the knees and elbows to see if they are still alive. Having done all this he can now log on to BrainSurgery.com with the handle DoctorYes and make appointments to treat all the brain surgery bottoms waiting to have their minds opened to the experiences they're sure they'll have because his bio says so.

Now Patrick thinks I should use Derek Shepherd, the neurosurgeon on *Grey's Anatomy*, as a better example, but you get my drift, I hope. If not, meet me in my dungeon and after I tie you up I'll use my single tail whip to discuss it with you.

So what do I want to say? It's pretty simple. Understand the actual process and explain it to others. Encourage them that we don't jump from fantasy to full-blown scene in one great leap. Remind them that there is more to what we do than costume and self-bestowed titles, that artistry comes only with practice and craftsmanship only after apprenticeship.

We all hated making those endless circles on three-line paper in first grade when we were learning to write. Yet without learning the basic skills, expert skills would never be attainable. We need to affirm that it takes more than attendance at demos to make a master. We need to know what the word master means. Look it up, as I did, and you'll see that master, as a verb, means "to become skilled or proficient in the use of;" as a noun: "an artist or performer of consummate skill."

In the long run the best of what we do is an art. Let's remember that and do our best to attain artistry for ourselves and all those who join us.

Role Models and Choices

April 23, 2007

I don't mind admitting that I've already made a large number of choices in my life. I've decided where to go to college, whom to marry, what to eat for dinner last Saturday night, where to live, to get divorced, whether or not to shower this morning, where to work, and, more recently (given the six decades during which I've been choosing), to become a professional writer.

Some decisions were easier than others, such as the decision not to shower (at least not before I finish my column), while others (like the divorce) were extremely difficult. Life is full of decisions both inconsequential and momentous.

I recently chatted with Brian, who is trying to make a life choice. As he admits, he is confused as to whether or not he wants to become someone's slave. He freely admits to longing to submit to a master, while experiencing a great deal of angst about the ramifications of making such a decision.

It's not an uncommon dilemma and, in fact, both relational and vocational choices are often difficult to make, especially when they include options that are as alternative as explicitly dominant/submissive relationships. I've come to believe that scene-related life choices are greatly clouded and hindered by a dearth of role models.

To be more precise, there aren't all that many men or women who present an accurate, viable, and widely available model of a healthy D/s long-term relationship. I'm not saying there are none, because I know quite a few of these excellent "role models" personally. The qualifier in the sentence before the last is that they are not readily available to the general public, nor even to most BDSM players.

On the other hand my opinion is that there are large numbers of people, both dominant and submissive, male and female, who continuously describe or display D/s models that are deficient in practicality, health, or viability as long term relationships. (I state it in those terms to differentiate it from strictly scene-related play, since a scene is certainly not a long term relationship.) What I mean is that there are many who don't know what they are talking about but talk about it anyway, thereby sowing disbelief, confusion, and apprehension in the minds of those considering a D/s lifestyle.

As usual, I'm going to remind you that the same applies to any fetish-laden lifestyle. Our detractors have the upper hand in this situation, since in most cases it's the crazies who get the publicity while healthy and wholesome practitioners often go unnoticed.

Before you jump all over me, I will happily admit that positive resources are available. Publishers, writers, teachers, vendors, event producers and the members of thousands of kinky groups, munches, and clubs do their best to disseminate information about the safe, sane, and consensual things that we do and relationships we live. Specific to my topic, Masters And slaves Together, both on national and local levels, and more than fifty (I've lost count) international master and slave titleholders, regional titleholders, and contestants offer sterling examples of healthy D/s.

Still we are a closeted and largely unseen subculture. Like homosexuals in the nineteen-forties and -fifties, we often try to "fly under the radar," hoping no one, especially police, politicians, and preachers, will notice what we do. What can I say? Not much except to admit to that reality and make my choices as best I can. I admit, too, that you have the same right -- fly under the radar, stay in the closet, and not present your healthy self as a positive role model. Still I will make bold to present three other suggestions.

Brian, look for healthy role models. Get off your butt, away from your keyboard, monitor, and CPU to meet real people who live the lifestyle you think you want. Find ways to debunk your brain of myth and hyperbole by learning the facts. Be sure those facts are seen, not heard. See for yourself rather than take others' words for what is true.

Let me clarify what I mean by this. In our culture, and here I especially mean Gay Leather, we often use the word "training" as a euphemism. Instead of bluntly saying that we want to play at being someone's slave, instead we advertise that we want training. I will grant that there can be, and often is, an important element of learning in our play. On the other hand, the euphemism masks the truth that we might very well benefit from training that is not in-and-of-itself play.

I'm not suggesting that you find a role model who will become your master. Instead I am saying find role models from whom you can derive a well-rounded and practical sense of the model you would use to fashion your life, whatever that might be. Look at it this way. You go to your own physician to be healed. He might or might not be a good role model, though I suspect if you go to him you think he is. He might not be the one, on the other hand, who would train you to become a doctor. In fact, there is a high probability that a physician who taught you would, on ethical grounds, refuse to treat you, except in emergency circumstances.

Get my point? First end your confusion by becoming educated, then set out to find the man or woman with whom you want to apply that education. In other words, the person who trains you to be a slave and therefore helps you understand yourself, slavery, and your slave self, may not become your master for life. It is as simple as that. Understand the difference between getting an education to make yourself proficient and living that proficiency.

To my friends, I say, "Take the risk to be a role model. Show the world, by your life, that what it is that we do is safe, sane, and consensual and just as importantly that we do nothing to be ashamed about, nothing that we need to hide."

And lastly, to those who have the courage and the ability to further Kink Liberation, it's time we build the institutions that will change society at large in its opinion of what it is that we do. Doing so will make it easier to find a role model and to be one. Let's form kinky credit unions, associations for sex positive and fetish aware doctors, lawyers, therapists, teachers, ministers, students, plumbers, gardeners, etc. Let's establish kinky libraries, schools, medical clinics, and especially political organizations that further sexually-related civil rights. Let's create caucuses in both the Democratic and Republican parties, as well as in the Greens, the Libertarians, and wherever else we are.

Where are the National Coalition of SSC Organizations, the National BDSM Speakers' Guild, the National Association of BDSM Retailers and Manufacturers? "Ollie, Ollie, All come free," I think is what we yelled when we were young and playing Hide and Go Seek. I know that it's time to "Come out, come out, wherever you are. One, two, three."

Only when we do will Brian and all those who are like him more easily find the role models needed to end their confusion.

The Three Ls of BDSM

December 16, 2006

There are lots of venues to meet kinky people, which leads us to negotiation, a usual necessity before we play. What we often fail to do is understand that good preparation is necessary for good negotiations. Recent overtures to experience "training" with me from several new-to-the-scene people have prompted me to think about what it takes to prepare for satisfactory negotiations.

I'm mindful of the question because I have had to negotiate with men who have no idea of what it means to negotiate, which simply reflects their lack of experience. What has happened each time, then, is that one of my initial questions, "What is your goal in playing with me?" was received with the reply "I don't know. I hadn't thought about that."

This essay, then, is my attempt to help all of us understand the fundamental reasons why we would negotiate with strangers. It seems to me that there are three basic reasons: lust, learning, and long term relationship (aka some kind of love). OK, Patrick would have me add "laughter." He's right. If we don't do it for fun, then perhaps we'd best not do it.

Now it's important that we notice a few attributes about each of these three rationales. First, of course, is that they are in no way exclusive of one another. In fact it is both probable and usual for us to negotiate for all of those reasons at the same time. Recognizing the three rationales helps us to tailor how we approach negotiations, especially as regards to the timetable that we are going to set. Additionally if we see ourselves in a particular way, the various rationales begin to take on more or less importance and therefore need to have a greater or lesser influence on what we negotiate. For example, if our reason is predominately lust we are going to have a faster timetable than if we are negotiating what we hope will be a long term relationship.

The first rationale, lust, is probably ever-present, even if we don't think of our desire for a scene to be a case of lusting. We don't, after all, often enter into negotiations with someone to whom we are not attracted. I will suggest that you note the caveat to that statement in the next rationale. Lust, rather than simply being one of the seven cardinal sins, is actually a strong motivator in the development of healthy, wholesome relationships that are going to have a sexual component. Face it. If it weren't for lust, there would be significantly fewer humans on this planet, perhaps including you and me.

Learning is an important rationale that ought to be embraced by all, but especially by those who are new to our subculture. I write "by all" because we ought never to stop learning. I negotiate, for instance, with strangers in order to play with them, and one of my hoped-for consequences is that I will get to know them better, which is to say that I will learn some things about them. The more I know about my potential partner, the more successful will be my future negotiations and my future play, be it short term or long. As Patrick says when he explains why I play with strangers, "Jack loves to explore." A new trick is a new experience that will hone my skills, teach me something about myself and my partner, and lead to a fuller, more-informed life.

Newbies are well-advised to make learning central to their purpose in negotiating and to make that purpose clear early in the discussion. There is, as I seem to write ad nauseam, no substitute for experience, an event that is fundamental to good learning. Here the term "learning" is quite inclusive. The scene will teach you about the fetish, about your partner, and most especially about yourself. Whether the scene is fun or not, it will still hold some kind of lesson. Better to know now what you don't like than to proceed in the dark. To learn that you've "Tried that but don't want to try it again" is an important lesson. Another important lesson in every scene is that experience tempers fantasy with reality.

I would also like to add that newbies are advised (and others should probably take note as well) that negotiating a long term relationship is best done, to say the least, only after there have been a series of successful short-term scenes. I am amazed at how many people fantasize about being in some kind of long term leather relationship well before they have any experience with the culture per se or (just as foolishly) with their potential partner. First, negotiate to learn, folks; then when you have an understanding of what we are about, you can turn your practiced negotiation skills towards finding Mr. or Ms. Right.

As a side note, be assured that most experienced players enjoy giving newbies experience for the sake of learning. In this regard, the lust component need not be present. Believe me, being flogged, for example, by someone who is not your type will still teach you a great deal about flogging, even if it's not a lusty experience.

And lastly, we all need to recognize the attraction that a long term relationship holds for us. None of us wants to be lonely and the sad fact is that many are attracted to our lifestyle because they see us as a welcoming community in which they can find both a place and a partner. There is, of course, no discounting an LTR as a rationale. What is important is to recognize how it fits into the scheme of negotiations.

To begin negotiations with a stranger on the basis of creating an LTR may be starting out on the wrong foot, especially if the love rationale is strongly linked to the lust rationale. Instead the learning rationale ought to be primary. Get to know one another. Learn about each other without the baggage of future expectations for an LTR. Play, experiment, experience with the freedom of not having a long term agenda. As you learn about one another, as you decide what you enjoy with mutual satisfaction and what you offer to one another in terms of support, pleasure, and talent, then you can allow the investigation of an LTR to take a greater role in your negotiations.

On the other hand, if a long-term relationship (LTR) is central to your negotiations, that should be initially stated and then tabled until the other rationales are more fully explored, namely that you have learned enough about one another and have found mutual satisfaction for your lust, so that you both know that there is the possibility of long-term living with one another, whatever that might entail.

For more details about the negotiation process itself, be sure to consult my website. In all of this, remember to proceed slowly, honestly, for mutual enjoyment, and of course for fun.

The Hunt for My Type

December, 1992

On a Sunday afternoon near Belmont and Halsted, my friend and I noticed that there sure were a lot of guys who were his "type." "That explains," he said, "why I look at so many of them with such lusty feelings."

Make no mistake about it, "typing" is a dangerous habit. It's certainly OK to pound away at a keyboard, but to fence yourself in with expectations and dream-filled descriptions of your next lover, master, or slave, is to enclose yourself in a deceit that will cause you to never find them. At least that's what my experience shows.

In 1985 I was steadily dating Steven, a man who was a wonderful friend and a great fuck buddy. But he wasn't my type. I was hoping, and waiting, just for Mr. Right: Six feet tall, handsome, Italian, educated, sophisticated, trim. Usually bottom, but could get dominant for a change of pace. A worldly-wise homebody. Add a great physique, smooth, clear skin. A party boy type.

That would be the man I could love, would love, forever. I actually knew the guy, too. I had met him about a year before and we had corresponded on occasion. I had gone to Provincetown twice to see him. He was my "type." In October of '85 the dream came true as Mr. Right agreed to move in with me. We started our relationship with five glorious days at Russian River. We were in love.

We returned home and settled in for a cozy winter. But Mr. Right (though he really is a wonderful guy) wasn't quite as Right as I had hoped. I had to get up at 6 am to go to work; he lounged around half the day and watched TV until all hours of the night.

I didn't like the idea of a closed relationship, but I agreed to it for him. He didn't like to go out as much as I did and thought most of my friends were boring and provincial.

In the meantime, of course, I had told Steven that our days of fucking were over. The truth was that they weren't.

Eight weeks into my new relationship I left Mr. Right at home and went on a weekend retreat where I roomed with "you know who" --- and we had great sex, even if Mr. Right wouldn't

19

have approved.

It was there that I realized that I loved Steven. Yes, I was attracted to my friend from Provincetown. And yes, he was better looking, more polished, taller, darker, and everything I thought I wanted in a man. But, truthfully, Steven was really the one I loved and who would, could, make me the happiest. He may not have been my type, but he was the one meant for me.

The day "Mr. Right" moved back to P'town, Steven moved in. From that day we shared more than five years as lovers.

* * * * *

There's another angle to this relationship hunt as well. Not only is our ideal type probably not the one we'll be happiest with, but very often we prevent the relationship from happening, all by ourselves, without his or her help. Let me illustrate with a story of more recent vintage.

Chuck left a message for me. Like a lot of guys just getting into the leather scene he wanted to know how to meet a master, one who would fulfill his ideal and dominate him to his heart's content. We talked a couple of times on the phone and I offered to give him an experience "on the bottom." After all, I was his type.

Chuck's visit started out really well, but in the end he left in a hurry and quite disappointed. He apologized for being a "failure" and before he left we talked about his feelings.

He knew that sex with me would mean that I would be in control. I made no bones about my thoughts on that matter. For his turn, Chuck thought that that would be a grand experience, until it actually happened.

Instead of the blissful feelings he thought he'd get, my style provoked a replay of his past. My voice, and the simple orders I gave him, reminded him too much of his parents' during his unhappy childhood. As is often the case, the realization of his fantasy just didn't come off as he had hoped.

I felt bad that Chuck didn't get the wonderful SM thrill he wanted, but I can't take responsibility for his childhood memories.

I'm not sure if I'll ever see Chuck again (though I'd like to) but if I do I'd like to discuss his search for a "master." That search is like the one for my type.

The simple truth is that if we want to be in a relationship which we presently don't have, we are confirming that we want things to change. We often fail to realize that to change things means we have to change the things over which we have control, but we only have real control over ourselves!

Ask yourself: What will be changed within me if I find (and get) the "type" I really want? Am I willing to make those changes to be in the relationship I think I desire? If my answer is "Yes," then what do I need to change in myself and how can I go about changing it?

You see, the best way to guarantee you meet "your type"

is to make yourself the other person's type. More often than not, the other person doesn't keep him or herself from us; we keep ourselves from them. I wasn't willing to change enough to keep "Mr. Right" but I didn't need to change at all for the man whom I really loved and who really loved me.

My Birthday Gift

March 12, 2007

People in our world often talk about rules and protocols and usually see them as being devised or imposed by the tops in our midst. A long time ago I learned that there is one rule that bottoms ought to follow stringently: Never give a top a toy you don't want him or her to use on you.

I learned that one day when a visiting bottom gave me a paddle (or at least I think that's what it was) and then complained when I spanked him with it. It seems really obvious to me that if he didn't want me to use it he should have left it at home, or at least have been smart enough to give me the gift only as he was leaving my home.

Sheesh! Sometimes it's way too noticeable that a guy is using his penis for a brain.

Let's fast forward to the twenty-first century. Patrick knew that I wanted another single-tail whip. My desire was very noticeable. At almost every vendor's table I looked for just the right one and if I found one I would pick it up, feel its weight, and swing it a bit. I'd feel the braids carefully and look over the workmanship. Too often the price tag was such that I'd put it down and walk away.

Last December, at the birthday dinner hosted for me, Patrick presented me with a most beautiful and carefully made signal whip. That is one long slim whip, about three feet in length. I prefer shorter whips as they are easier to control and there is limited swinging room in my dungeon.

In giving me such a gift, Patrick was breaking the rule I just stated, as he really doesn't like being whipped, especially if the hits are on his back. In his defense I have to say that in this case his love and devotion were more important than his dread of the whip. He gave the gift not for his tastes but for my desire.

Good scenes and good friendships have that in common. When we do something for the other person, instead of for ourselves, the event is doubly enhanced. It's ironic that selflessness can sometimes be the most direct path to selfish satisfaction. Now there's a sentence that takes some thought if you want to make sense of it.

Look at it this way. By selflessly giving me a gift that he

might not want to give, Patrick gained the greater satisfaction of knowing that he had given me what I had really desired.

I took my present and hung it with my whips and paddles. It stayed there more than three months before I used it. I was waiting for the right moment, since a good whipping takes both time and place. At this month's Hellfire party, I decided it was the right time and place. After we had both finished our volunteer duties, I grabbed my toy bag, found Patrick and looked for a vacant St. Andrews cross. Using leather wrist and ankle cuffs I spread his naked body on the cross.

Admittedly he was bound rather loosely, not that he could get away but rather that he could do a lot of squirming. I like to see him squirm. In fact causing groans and squirms of pain are among my favorite pastimes. Making skin turn pink to red to blue is fun too. Only a sadist can really understand that phenomenon. It's not the infliction of pain that turns me on. It's the results that it causes. In fact, I prefer bottoms who can't stand pain. Real masochists take way too much work! Wimps are much easier to hurt.

Of course it's not fair to call'em wimps, but you get the idea. They're not wimps, you see, if they are willing to do that which they hate just to turn me on.

For a change I put some effort into Patrick's ordeal. I started out with an easy flogging, though not with a real gentle flogger. From there I progressed to a crop, a paint stirrer, and finally my birthday gift.

The new whip worked well as I just brushed Patrick's now pink back with its thin braid. It really was a teasing sensation, as I knew he was dreading what was to come. Quite frankly, since it is a new whip I took it more gently than I might have if I knew how to wield it with more expertise and if my bottom was really into heavy, bloody pain.

No matter. I had a really good time and was proud to show off my slave's devotion. I like playing with Patrick in public as an affirmation of our relationship. Private scenes are much more common since there we have a freedom to let loose as well as to be intimate without distraction.

In due time the squirms were coming on hot and heavy. I paused my whipping now and then to feel the heat of his flesh and to caress his body. The gift of the whip was now a gift that was giving again. Is it no wonder that I consider myself so blessed?

It wasn't one of those-whip-to-blood scenes and it needn't be. I got what I wanted well before I had to "let loose." The whipping was never as intense as it could have been. I had no desire to go there. If I had, the bondage would have been more complete; there would have been no wiggle room on the cross. Patrick would have been bound tightly so that the target of his back would have been immovably secure, a place to lash out with directness until his tender skin began to ooze and then bleed.

But sadism doesn't have to go that far to be erotic. It only has to know its power and its control. The slave was mine and he had shown that with the gift, quietly tendered in a fancy restaurant in the heart of Washington, DC and now shown to our Leather brothers at the clubhouse.

Too often we fail to see the importance of giving in what we do, that BDSM is not a mindless act of desire, but rather it is more correctly seen as the gift of self. The best of what we do is the gift of both selves. It is not only bottoms who are called to give. Tops, too, must give of themselves by freely being who they are. It is a strange idea that I can best please Patrick only by being the selfish, sadistic, and demanding son of a bitch that I am. It is only by taking what I want, Patrick on the cross as an example, that gives him what he truly wants.

Strange bedfellows we make, but happy ones to be sure.

Doing It

Dungeon Etiquette

June 27, 2008

My friend Master Z of Chicago is putting together a beginner's package for attendees to Kinky Kollege and Sinsations In Leather so he asked me for a column on this topic. I'm happy to oblige him. As an aside let me note that I always give people permission to repost and/or reprint my columns as long as they don't omit or change anything in them including my copyright, my URL and my email address. So if you want this for your organization's use you may have it, though I hope you will still ask me for permission.

I'll begin with a few general suggestions because everything you really need to know boils down to using common sense. On the other hand, in today's world, common sense seems to be anything but common. Therefore let me make bold to remind you that what you see and hear among us, must stay right there. Naming names, telling stories "out of school," and just general gossip is not socially-acceptable behavior, in or out of the dungeon.

On the other hand, if you see something that deserves a comment, such as unsafe play or illegal activity, tell those responsible for the safety, legality, and appropriateness of the space. Let them deal with it. Unless there's some kind of emergency, there's rarely a reason for you to do so.

Newcomers to our subculture can be easily overwhelmed by our language, dress, and activities. I know, since I once felt like a kid in a candy store. Knowing what to do and what not to do poses a myriad of questions about how to act and what to think.

So "When in Rome, do as the Romans do." Learn what is the usual practice and follow it. If you don't know what the usual practice is, then ask. Asking is always the safer course and doing so makes you sound smart, no matter how stupid you think the question is. Another good way to figure out the local practices is to read their dungeon rules. They are often posted on the wall or in their program book. If they're not, then ask where you can find them.

My mom would add lots of other clichés here, such as: "Look before you leap;" "It's better to be seen than to be heard;" "Listen first then speak." "Avoid the appearance of being a "Know it all," even if you are the most experienced player in the room. In every case humility is a real advantage. Remember, as my mom would never let me forget, that "While you're under my roof, you'll do as I say." Dungeon rules, suggestions, protocols or laws (call them what you like) are going to vary immensely from space to space. Believe me, what you can do in Seattle ain't going to fly in lots of other cities. Therefore go with the flow in the space you're in, not the flow that works somewhere else.

Play safely. Doing so probably means that you need to arrive ready to play safely, i.e., bring your own condoms and lube, etc., though to be honest penetration isn't allowed in very many public spaces. If it is allowed it's likely that only certain kinds of insertion will be permissible. I know. I know. I can't figure out why you can sometimes fuck with a dildo but not with a prick. Thank god that dungeon masters don't patrol hotel guest rooms. Safely also means that you remain a safe distance from whipping scenes. That whip master, after all, wants to hit his or her bottom, not yours.

Which reminds me that in every case I've ever seen, the Dungeon Master (DM) is the ultimate authority, so do as he says. What will he or she say?

Keep your socializing in the social area. That means that conversations shouldn't be held in the play space. Take them elsewhere.

Illegal activity, such as recreational drug use, prostitution, and bestiality, have no place in our places.

Watch but don't touch. The intimate activity that the voyeur in you admires so well is just that: Intimate. Don't intrude or disturb. When both the play and the aftercare are obviously over, then you can politely ask questions, give compliments, or even see if they'll give you a similar experience.

Touching also applies to anything that's not yours: toys, tools, equipment, such as floggers, ropes, chains, restraints, slave girls and boys, and all the rest. I know you learned that in kindergarten but reminders never hurt.

Don't be an equipment hog. Stated otherwise, if people are waiting to use what you're using, take your turn and let them have theirs. As a rule, an hour is more than sufficient for a scene so don't take longer, unless no one is waiting. When in doubt ask the DM.

By the way, that hour? It includes cleaning up after yourself. You've heard your mom tell you what mine told me: "Clean up after yourself. I'm not your maid" and ""When you're done with it put it back where you found it." This also means to clean the equipment as well. No one wants to play in your sweat, tears, or other body fluids.

Be courteous, kind and welcoming. Does someone appear to be a newcomer? Show them around; show them the rules; and make them feel at home.

Dress appropriately coming to and from the place where the play is held. As my Leather forefathers said "Don't scare the natives." As we say these days, "Be street legal." The idea is that you don't want to attract undue attention to the group and its activities.

Though it's not something you're liable to see posted on the wall nor told in an orientation class, don't confuse roles or status. Unless some other kind of relationship has been clearly negotiated, we are all equals. A master is master to his or her slave only. Likewise being one person's slave, miss, boy, maid or puppy doesn't make you everyone else's. If you feel your rights are being violated then consult with the DM.

In the meantime get yourself one or two introductory books on what it is that we do (WIITWD). In no time at all you'll feel included. Welcome to our lifestyle.

An Intro Course in Bondage

January 15, 1997

Becoming an expert in bondage techniques takes experience. You're not going to get from here to "there" in one easy step, but you will get there with practice, information, experience, and the right equipment. Starting out is merely getting the fundamental tools and starting where you are. You'll hear me say time and time again that you don't have to do anything with great expense or "whole hog." It's best to start out small and slow. You'll have lots of time later for big investments and marathon bondage sessions.

So come with me this morning as I walk through my local Ace Hardware and see how we can put together a rope kit for Bondage 101. The names of the equipment may vary from supplier to supplier. The numbers in parentheses reflect suburban hardware rates.[1] You can probably get things cheaper if you try.

I'm going to start off with a good pair of scissors. Ideally you'll get the kind used to remove bandages after surgery. They have dull ends so that the skin is safe while you cut your bottom loose. You'll probably have to make a quick stop at a pharmacy to get these. I mention scissors first because in all this bondage stuff, as in all SM, safety comes first. Never tie someone up without a pair of good scissors nearby in case of an emergency.

That said, our next stop is for rope. There are two types that I use: clothesline and nylon. Pick up a 50-foot package of 7/32 inch by 100 feet ($5.79) cotton rope. Cut it into variable lengths between 7 and 18 or so feet. You'll want to have shorter lengths for some things such as tying feet, wrists, or cocks, and longer for others, such as around chests and arms or thighs. Once cut, you may want to protect the ends from fraying. Nylon cord is easy to melt with a candle's flame. Heat it enough so that it begins to melt and then form it into a secure end.

You'll have to be a bit more creative with the frayed ends of clothesline. I immersed the ends of my first ropes in glue and then let the glue dry by setting the ropes' ends on wax paper. Be sure the glue (I used Elmer's) soaks into the rope. Rubber cement

30   1 Please be advised that these reflect 1997 prices. Expect to pay more.

works, but not as well. To be real fancy, you could wrap the ends with thin twine or fish line. Wind it around the ends tightly and evenly so that it doesn't snag or slip off.

At this point I'll refer you to a Boy Scout handbook or a book on knot tying. Of course it's not a bad idea to get one of those anyway, though many bondage enthusiasts will readily admit that they use only a few standard knots.

Cotton clothesline is my favorite rope because it ties easily and is flexible, though it tends to get dirty and sometimes the knots can be more difficult to untie.

Nylon, on the other hand, seems to stay cleaner and is easier to loosen. The down side to this is that nylon knots tend to loosen too easily. You can get it in various thicknesses [¼ ($6.79), 3/8 ($13.79), ½ ($23.47) inch for instance] and lengths (the prices are for 50 feet). I prefer the 3/8 inch ropes. Thinner is more dangerous, thicker is harder to work with. In any case, among these three choices it's probably more a question of esthetics than safety, as long as you tie knots safely in the first place.

Avoid twine, fishing line, any thin rope or thread, and any rope made of a rough material such as jute or manila. Leather thongs are nice if used with care. Be mindful that the thinner the cord, the more liable it is to cut or otherwise damage skin. Thin cords are more dangerous too in that they will more easily cut off your bottom's circulation.

An exception might be the use of nylon twine ($2.19 for 260 feet) where you use lots of twine to weave your bondage around your bottom. Here I emphasize weaving as opposed to tying per se, though it may be just a matter of terminology. If the tying is done so that the twine remains snug enough to stay but loose enough so as not to constrict, the bondage can be a real work of art. The details for such artistry, though, are beyond an intro course. Mentioning it is just food for thought.

Ropes aren't the only tools for tying. Chains and lashing straps are somewhere to be found in every hardware store. A pair of 9 foot straps ($4.79) would be useful for bondage to a cross, chair, or sawhorse or to secure a bottom's arms to his or her chest. There's a use for stretch cords if you have the place for them. Lengths of 24, 32, and 46 inches range in cost from $2 to $3.00.

The next stop at Ace's is to the aisle where they sell chain. Quarter inch coil chain is $1.59 per foot. Unless you want to invest in a pair of cutters, know your required lengths before you buy them. Add an inch or so to your measurements as it's always better to have it too long than too short.

With the chains you'll also need bolt snaps ($1.59 each). These are double-ended snaps and you'll never need fewer than the number you buy. I guess I own more than a couple of dozen and I still find myself in a scene looking for another one. For more permanent attachment use a quick link for under 50 cents.

31

Chain can serve several purposes. It certainly works as a bondage material, though you'll want to get leather restraints to attach your bottom to the chain. It's not as comfortable as rope but it does pose less danger. Here again it's a matter of taste and the kind of scene you're both into.

More often chain serves as a great point of attachment. You can, for instance, run a length of chain around the edge of your bed and then tie your bottom spread eagle on the bed. Each link serves as a point of attachment. The nice thing about an arrangement such as this is that the equipment is portable, storable, easily hidden, and usable without altering furniture or walls.

I'm thinking of a scene where the chain encircles the bed and the bottom is loosely encased in nylon twine, Gulliver in Lilliputian style. Yards of twine would go from link to leg and back again, link to chest, link to arm, etc. Sounds hot to me. I'll have to try that on Matthew.

I haven't even started on locks and screw eyes, nor on Saran wrap or duct tape. Some things, I guess, need to be left to your imagination or the next essay.

Where To Tie

January 22, 1997

Once we're past the "tie with what" question we're faced with the "tie to what" dilemma. The answers demand more creativity. Today's answers will focus on more novice-like solutions. Just because I'm not going to mention a bondage box built into the wall of your 16x20 foot dungeon doesn't mean that you can't use it for restraining your bottom.

My purpose, though, is to give advice of an introductory nature, so if your experience levels are way beyond these bounds, use the column as a refresher, not a complete guide.

"Tying to" breaks down into two categories: first is to tie the bottom to himself, such as one wrist to another wrist; second is to tie him or her to some other object, such as a chair or hook. Tying one bottom to another bottom spans both those categories.

The first alternative, bottom to him or herself, is certainly the one that takes the least amount of equipment. Rope and chain around flesh or clothes can be its own erotic presentation.

As you bind your partner keep several safety points in mind: Never tie so as to constrict the flow of blood. Either make your knots loose enough to be safe or make them in such a way as to insure that the rope is sufficiently spaced. Putting inner wrist to inner wrist, for instance, and then tying around both wrists is a good way to bind safely.

Never, of course, tie anything around the neck, obstruct the nasal passages, nor gag completely.

Your bottom's position is also a safety factor. Never leave a person tied face down in a prone position. Never support your partner solely with ropes or chains unless the restraints are more than amply strong and the body is fully and safely supported by adequate harnesses.

Be mindful of your bottom's position, even if they are standing or sitting. Elevated arms or legs, strained muscles or joints, and flimsy equipment all pose dangers, especially in the long run. Along similar lines remember that a person who is struggling, excited, angry, or afraid can exercise strength much greater than we might suppose. One of the reasons we use bondage, such as in a whipping session, is to insure that the bottom can

33

struggle safely. The last thing you want is a boy who is flailing left and right. Bondage that is too loose may cause rope burns as well.

You'd best use your imagination or an old copy of *Bound and Gagged* for ideas on tying wrists to ankles, wrists to knees, cocks to feet, elbows to knees and wrists to ankles, etc. Remember though that some of the things you see in photos are well-staged but not practical.

The over-riding principle in any bondage scene is to check with your bottom often to insure that all is going well. Let him or her know to warn you of impending danger, such as numbness or dizziness. It's up to you, too, to check to see that no body parts (i.e., feet and hands) cool off, a sign of restricted circulation.

Intro to bondage assumes that you want to use what's handy for equipment. In the long run you'll build or acquire more elaborate bondage gear such as sawhorse, dog cage, or restraint table. But what's a beginner to do?

Look around. Use a footstool, straight back chair, bed, desk, table, toilet, or staircase railing. All of these offer innocuous and practical points for attaching, depending upon your purpose.

Chairs work well for bondage for the sake of bondage or to tie your partner for a tickling session, genital torture, or nipple play. A bed is more conducive to whipping his or her back or for fucking. A low stool and a bed with a foot board combine very well. Perhaps you could lay a chair on its back to restrain your partner on the floor.

My good friend Vince has an eye-hook in a beam in the ceiling of his living room. When his mother asked about it, he simply said that he thought it was used by a previous occupant for hanging a plant.

So my discussion quietly moves into eye hooks. If you have the luxury of inserting them into your home, be sure to anchor them securely, use appropriately large sizes, and pre-drill the holes, being sure that the holes aren't too large. Again, the rule about over-building applies.

There are a number of discreet places to insert eye-hooks without raising your landlord's ire, such as inside a closet.

When I lived in a studio apartment I built a frame of two by fours that fit into the doorway between the bedroom and bathroom. By clamping one board to another no nails or screws defaced any part of the building.

Later I went to a metal working shop and had the craftsman make me a heavy gamma-shaped hook that fit over the top of a closet door. It is of thin gauge steel with a ring welded to one side. Hang it over the door, shut the door, and it becomes a very effective place to which you can attach your partner.

To give your partner a fuller bondage experience, try mummification. Though it is best done with an assistant, two people (the top and the bottom) can perform it.

First of all, gather your equipment: plastic wrap, duct tape, Ace bandages, balls of cotton, a large towel, and of course those scissors.

Have your partner stand at the foot of the bed facing away with hands behind the neck. Begin by wrapping his arms and chest; as you reach the nipples place a piece of cotton between them and the wrap. Once the armpits are covered, have her lower her arms and encase the arms against the torso. Once the upper body is encased you can then begin on his or her legs. You may want to use a hood or cover the eyes with an Ace bandage.

Now comes the tricky part. Spread the towel on the bed. Standing behind your partner, gently and carefully lean him or her down onto the bed. If he or she is larger than you, you'll see why the assistant is helpful. When the person is prone you can get fancier with the wrap, covering the feet, for example, or the head. Be certain that there is plenty of breathing room and that the mouth and nose hole is quite large and unencumbered.

Now I would use the scissors to cut holes to expose the tits. The cotton helps to make sure you don't cut skin. Likewise I free the genitals for play. After all, most of my bondage is for the sake of later play!

You can get still fancier by covering the wrap with duct tape, creating a complete mummification scene. Be sure to monitor your bottom's progress and vital signs. Never leave such a person, or any person in bondage, unattended.

Excuse me, I have to go check up on Patrick's ropes.

Leather Restraints

January 29, 1997

As my friend David pointed out, I haven't yet mentioned leather restraints: "Some very practical applications of bondage, thanks. I was surprised that you didn't mention pre-made wrist/ankle restraints as part of the scene, [as] they are easier to attach than plain rope for the novice & just as effective. Just my ideas," he writes via e-mail.

Good ideas too, but I was saving them for last. It's my advice to start your toy collection slowly and cheaply. That reflects my pocketbook, of course, but I'm probably not too much poorer than most of my readers.

The first leather purchase I would advise has nothing to do with bondage. Get yourself a bar vest (priced as low as $29.00, but more usually between $60.00 and $100.00), as it's the equipment that's most necessary and the piece that's the least easy to make yourself.

Most everything else I'm going to list today can be homemade. Take a walk around a Tandy leather store. My first leather restraints were made from remnants purchased in a "grab bag" for a dollar. The necessary tools and buckle don't cost much more. Making it yourself is a great way to spend these cold winter nights, when the wind chill (that make-believe number that the weather people use in order to make their news more newsworthy) is low enough to keep you home. Besides, spreading a piece of leather out on the kitchen table is a great way to tell your lover that you want to start a new hobby!

Enough jokes, Jack.

The first leather toy, then, is a pair of wrist restraints. They come in either buckle or D-ring varieties. The buckle types are self-contained. The D-rings allow you to use padlocks. Some buckles can be locked as well and some restraints come with locking posts. Wrist restraints, as most leather toys, come padded or unpadded. The major difference between the two has to do with utility. If you are going to have long-term or more strenuous bondage scenes, the padding can be very helpful, even imperative. For ease of use and carrying convenience, the plain ones work well. ($40 unlined, $69 padded)

You'll have to shop around to find your favorite Leather toy retailer. There are several online, and most larger cities have at least one. You can also find toys at the vending area of any Leather weekend.

With the restraints you'll want to make sure you have those bolt snaps mentioned in part one. Leather restraints have the advantage of being safer, since constriction is more easily avoided. Still, be careful to check extremities for circulation.

An important safety note is to keep your locks locked so that you have to unlock them in order to use them. Doing so insures that you have the key handy when and where you need it. Ankle restraints are a bit bigger than wrist ones ($49 to $79). Some come with attached chains, a nice feature. A set of ankle and wrist restraints serves well as the basic bondage kit, as it is useful for the spread-eagle position we all favor.

For playing with males, I would next go for cock and ball restraints. There are a myriad of varieties of stretchers, separators, and sheaths, too numerous to list here, but be sure to include figure eights to go around the nuts and cock and two-snap ball stretchers to pull the testicles away from the cock. Parachutes are a favorite of mine. They encircle the nuts leaving small chains dangling for the easy attachment of weights or cords. Eventually you'll want to buy weights as well. You'll have to experiment with your bottom's tolerance. Start easy and add weight as you see how much his nuts can take. Eight to ten pounds isn't unheard of. I've even seen a photo (was it real or Memorex?) of much more weight being lifted by the scrotum, but caution and reason is necessary here. I don' want anyone going to the emergency room saying that "Jack sent me."

Thigh and wrist restraint combos ($119) are straps that go just where you think, fastening the arms at the side and out of the way. Up in the neck department, collars, again in a wide variety, sell for $30 to $65. Some have D-rings for attaching wrists to neck, some come with wrist straps already attached. The variations are endless.

A simple Ace bandage is sufficient for blindfolding, but you can get fancier with a leather blindfold ($25-$39). Jon, the manager of Eagle Leathers, once showed me a great blindfold made of latex. It was inflatable. Now there's a neat present. More on latex later.

To get fancier in the blindfold department, you can get a spandex hood ($20). The advantage of spandex is that you can breathe through it and see shadows. Spandex hoods come off very easily and quickly, just the kind of thing to use with a novice. He won't be spooked by total darkness. Later, of course, you'll want to put a leather hood over it, but these are more expensive ($115 or so). Again the varieties of hoods are endless. I prefer the kind with open mouths, since I love to use a bottom's mouth. They come with detachable gags and blindfolds, and some have

D-rings.

In a similar category, a head harness acts much like a hood except that much more of the head is exposed. I like to immobilize my bottom with it. He can hear, see, and use his mouth, but his head can't otherwise move, once I've attached the harness to the ceiling, cross, bed, or bondage box.

Harnesses come in chain and leather ($45 to $149) and encircle the torso in a number of ways. By and large you will find them strictly decorative, though there's nothing wrong with dressing for the part.

At this point, I'd suggest you get a hold of a catalogue ($20) from Mr. S Leathers (www.mr-s-leather.com). You can tell them that Jack sent you. Seeing pictures of all this gear will explain it much better than even my writing can do. Besides, the people at Mr. S have great-looking models. Ladies should ask about Madame S Leathers, their sister store.

I suggest the catalogue (I mean to get one) because the visual presentation really does explain a lot. Not every novice has to learn only by doing or having done. That said, I'll recommend a few books: **The Master's Manual, A Handbook of Erotic Dominance** by Jack Rinella, Daedalus Publishing, ISBN 1-881943-03-8, $14.95; **Learning The Ropes** by Race Bannon, Daedalus Publishing, ISBN 1-881943-07-0, $12.95; **Leathersex** by Joseph Bean, Daedalus Publishing, ISBN 1-881943-05-4 $14.95; and **Leatherman's Handbook II** by Larry Townsend, Carlyle Communication, ISBN 0-503-09999-6, $5.95.

As I promised, a quick note about latex bondage, with a nod to my friend Ryan Johnson. Depending upon the size of your bottom, three to six rolls of latex make a great mummification wrap. The rolls are 4 inches wide by 16 feet ($20 each). They make immobility easy, though not inexpensive. Latex is a great turn-on and very versatile, though you really have to take care of it and learn a few of the do's and don'ts.

Other possibilities, well beyond intro bondage, are leather straight jackets, sleep sacks, and suspension equipment (from $200 up, and I mean UP). All I've ever been able to afford is to look, but it sure looks good. This kind of bondage, though, takes expertise, both on the part of the top and the bottom. Make sure you've graduated with honors from Intro and Intermediate before you go for the gold.

Healthy SM

July 21, 1996

Since my essay on raunch (see page 73) side-steps the issues of health, it's only fair that I write about safer sex practices[1] somewhere in this book.

When I came into the Leather world in 1983, AIDS was still a mystery, few if anyone had any facts about it, and Gay men were dying left and right. That fearful period had been preceded by a "glory time" of rampant sex, since modern science had seemed to reduce sexually transmitted diseases (STDs) by and large to a mere inconvenience solved by a shot of penicillin. Well, twenty years later, things have changed a great deal, though not always for the better.

Let me give my usual disclaimer here: I am not a medical doctor so I can only give you what I know, without the comfort that my information is absolutely correct. That said, I will remind you that you need to discuss the issue of STDs with your primary care physician, including the fact that you practice sadomasochistic sex. If you are too embarrassed to do that, find another doctor with whom you are more comfortable.

You might also get somewhat more reliable information from your local health department or (if you live somewhere that you disbelieve that statement) from the health department in a nearby larger city. You can also find good information from one of the many health centers, such as Howard Brown in Chicago (http://www.howardbrown.org/hb_resources.asp) or the San Francisco Department of Public Health (http://www.dph.sf.ca.us/DPHMenu.htm). In any case the primary rule for staying healthy is to be well-informed. Many people miss this point and err on the side of denial (refusing to think about it at all), or on the side of hubris (thinking that they have all the facts and don't need any more). I will grant you that no one has all the answers, including yours truly, but that is no reason not to have some of the answers, especially since there are enough reliable answers that you can stay free of disease, if you follow the generally acceptable guidelines.

As in all things, STD safety demands common sense.

1 This article doesn't take into account any recent changes in medical practices, though it seems to me that it remains valid information.

Nothing is absolutely guaranteed. I say that because it is true. Healthy SM doesn't mean no SM; healthy sex doesn't mean no sex. Nothing is totally safe but that doesn't mean that you can't make something safer. Inform yourself, then, so that you can reduce risk and play more safely.

Well-informed play is what is necessary and that means that your information needs to be up-to-date and rather thorough. Consider both the source and the breadth of the data. Getting your information from your buddies, for instance, may not make your play safer.

Healthy SM is as much a case of cleanliness as anything else. Learn how to clean your toys so that they are disease free. Keeping ropes, slings, whips, gags, dildoes and the like clean is matter of doing so. There's nothing expensive about soap and water. Rinsing insertable toys in bleach (diluted in water in a ration of one to ten) is highly recommended as well. Leather toys may not stand up to washing like a butt plug would, but there are ways to disinfect them as well. See *Leather And Latex Care: How To Keep Your Leather And Latex Looking Great* by Kelly Thibault, (ISBN 1-881943-00-3, Daedalus Publishing Co.)

The other basic concept is to avoid sharing bodily fluids, though, quite frankly, even this notion has changed over the years. HIV, for instance, seems not to be transmitted orally. That said, there is the important caveat that it's not transmitted orally in a healthy mouth. If you have bleeding gums, then it can be transmitted through the mouth, but not through kissing. On the other hand, healthy gums seem to be a protective barrier against the spread of HIV, as is unbroken skin.

But healthy sex is more than just avoiding HIV. Other STDs are more easily contracted, even orally. The solution is to know your own health status and that of your partner. Here's where your doctor comes in. Sexually active players need to be routinely checked for disease, certainly once a year. This checkup will be automatic if you've been forthright with your doctor. If you don't see your doctor for a yearly checkup, then you are not playing safe. Players ought to be tested for HIV, Hepatitis, as well as other STDs. You need also to be vaccinated against Hepatitis, if you haven't already become immune to it. Again this is something to discuss with your physician.

Healthy sex means that you are prepared to play safely. Having disinfectants handy, using condoms, and discussing health factors when you negotiate are just some of the ways to preserve your good health and the health of those with whom you play or who will play in the same space after you. That, by the way, is a strong hint to clean up after yourself.

SM is, and should always be, an adult activity. In spite of the plethora of fantasies, roles, and play, there is no safe SM without responsibility. Stated otherwise, irresponsible behavior has no place in our kinky lifestyle, our dungeons, our relationships, or our play. Staying healthy is your responsibility and it is one that you should not ignore. Being responsible means that you ask the difficult questions of your partner about his or her health, that you take time to learn the pertinent facts about the transmission of disease and the prevention of injury, and that you not only learn the facts but that you practice them. As regards practice, it is important to avoid those situations where your will to resist unsafe sex is diminished. Spelling out that dictum means that you avoid substances (alcohol and drugs) that will make you less likely to play safely.

It also means that you don't assume basic facts about safer sex or your partner. Ask, if you don't know. Yes, it can be difficult to ask personal questions about matters of health, but it is your health that is at risk. Just because you live in a small town doesn't mean that you are immune to disease. Just because you are afraid of your potential partner's response is no reason not to ask.

Being pro-active to keep yourself healthy, after all, is the best solution to remaining healthy.

Preaching to the Choir

July 07, 2006

The death of a Leatherman in Lynn, Massachusetts prompted several requests for me to write about scene safety. For those of you who haven't heard, the story is this, though I need to remind you that I am not a forensic expert and I don't know what really happened. It seems that Adrian Exley of London, England, met Gary Leblanc of Lynn, Massachusetts through an internet cruising site. Adrian was into rubber, latex, and breath control. Gary, a top, was as well. When Adrian failed to return home as scheduled, his sister contacted the police in Lynn. Adrian had left information about where he was going. Lynn police eventually questioned Gary, who committed suicide the next day. Adrian's body was found buried in a Rhode Island park.

It is a sad story that might never have happened, if the two players had played safely. We don't know what went wrong. We do know, though, how to plan so that things go more right than wrong. We can never insure a completely safe scene. What we can do is to play in such a way as to mitigate the risks, reducing them to what is a safe level. People drown in bathtubs, which is still not sufficient reason to refrain from bathing. What, on the other hand, can we do to minimize danger?

Beware of the loner. This is not a caution that only applies to your partner. It applies to you as well. Are you a loner? Do you have to meet people secretly? Are you involved in a supportive community that will help protect you from yourself, one that will teach you safer sex and safer scene techniques? Or do you have the foolish belief that you can go it alone, that you don't need to be taught?

Worse yet, do you think you can actually learn safety over the Internet? Do you think that fiction and fantasy are suitable substitutes for learning from an experienced player? Do you ignore the basics of good safety, thinking you are too smart to need to learn them? Do you think you can be an expert because you act like one? If you do, then you are the one who is dangerous. You are dangerous to yourself.

Yes, being wary of the loner applies to your partner as well, which leads me to the next piece of advice on safety: Check references. Referencing is one of the oldest and best precautions we can learn from those folks we call the Old Guard. If your partner has no references, then it is best that you realize that he or she may have a bad reputation, is a loner, or is a beginner.

Now don't get me wrong. I like beginners but I also know that I can only play with beginners at a beginner's level. If you are a beginner it behooves you to find experienced partners and to inform them that you are a beginner. In such an arrangement you'll not only be safe, but you will quickly and correctly soon lose your beginner's status.

For some strange reason, the logic of the last paragraph evades many beginners. As an experienced player (nearly 25 years in the scene) I'm amazed when newbies tell me they won't play with me because I have "too much experience." Those quotation marks, as incredible as they seem, are for real. I've been given that line of malarkey more than once. In fact, the opposite is true. Newbies should avoid, in most cases, other newbies.

OK, got that? The phrase "in most cases" leads us to the next rule of safety. Public play, in a properly equipped and staffed space, is the safest form of play. A properly staffed space has a trained dungeon monitor who knows how to gauge the quality and safety of a scene, knows what to do in case of an emergency, and is able to facilitate not only safe but enjoyable scenes as well.

Herein lies our communal responsibility. We players must design, implement, and avail ourselves of proper DM training, which includes more than just knowing how to walk around wearing an orange vest. It includes first aid, knowledge of where equipment is kept, dungeon etiquette, and "reading" the signs of a scene to insure that what is happening is safe, sane, and consensual. For our part, we need to respect the DM's role.

From here then we need to insure that our private spaces match the safety levels of our public ones. Do you have the proper equipment in your bedroom? Now I can only guess what you do there, but I can ask if you have what you need to insure that if something goes wrong you can fix it quickly and completely. This may be something as simple as condoms and water soluble lubricant, as a good pair of scissors to cut off plastic wrap and duct tape, or keys that actually work in the locks you are using. My point is that when there is no dungeon monitor, we all have to become dungeon monitors.

We have to police ourselves. Do you let alcohol and drugs increase your danger? Is your equipment strong enough to use the way you want to use it? Have you taken proper precautions with heaters, candles, and needles?

Several years ago I invested in a tens unit for electrical play. The vendor who sold it to me gave me a guided tour of its use, but when I finally did use it, Patrick came to the conclusion that I didn't have the skill level necessary to use it on him. He was right and the unit remains on the shelf. No matter how dominant or submissive you are, you can never give up your responsibility to do your best to insure that a scene is safe. No amount of lust, fantasy, or desire replaces the need for safety, sanity, and consent.

You can argue forever about your freedom, your preference for risk aware consensual kink (RACK), or the willingness you have to take risks. None of those things gives you the right to be irresponsible, either with your life or someone else's.

And lastly, remember that accidents do happen. When they occur, appeal for help. The closet is no substitute for a call for help. Embarrassment is a small price to pay for aid.

Have fun, folks, but do so with a proper education.

A Primary Technique

May 07, 2006

The slap on our ass that induces our first breath may not be the first SM event that we experience, but inhaling is certainly the most important first act of a newborn and one that will be repeated consistently throughout his or her life. There is nothing more natural than breathing and I suggest that you all continue to do so for as long as you can.

Besides its life-sustaining properties, though, breathing is an important technique in sexual activity in general and SM play specifically. Of course if you stop breathing that generally ends the scene and the fun, but kidding aside, breathing, or I should say "proper breathing" adds immensely to the pleasure of what it is that we do.

Let me wander off topic for a moment and note that I've never heard of a seminar on proper breathing techniques at any BDSM educational conference. My solution? Let's invite La Maze experts to teach us how to breathe when we play, since the utilization of proper breathing techniques can enhance WIITWD[1] in several ways. They will increase endurance, so we can do it longer; they will help induce an altered state; and they will facilitate closer bonding between partners.

Though we seldom do more than joke about it, topping can be real work. I freely admit, for instance, that my arm often gives out from flogging or spanking sooner than the ass or back on the bottom being hit. Proper breathing techniques will increase the supply of oxygen to the muscles in my arm. They will also help me to maintain a rhythm that will better sustain my continuing. The right pace will slow me down, thereby extending my impact time significantly. The longer the time between impacts, the more time for endorphins to take effect in my bottom and the more powerful the scene.

The use of proper breathing techniques is even more important when it comes to the player on the bottom side of the scene. Here I will note that I was actually taught to breathe by the tops who introduced me to sadomasochistic activity. One-on-one mentoring, after all, does have something going for it.

I will also note, though, that my appreciation for good

1 What it is that we do.

breathing comes from two non-SM sources. First, as the husband of an expectant mother, I attended La Maze classes. Here I learned breathing exercises and techniques that effectively mitigate the pain of childbirth. In La Maze the father-to-be learns the same things the mom-to-be is taught and is then encouraged to prompt and support his wife's application of those exercises before and during delivery.

Just as those techniques mitigate the pain of delivery, they can do the same for the pain received during a scene. In both cases there are several methodologies at work here. Part of what is happening is that concentration on your breathing distracts you from the pain itself, since thinking about what hurts will make it hurt (or seem to hurt) more. Secondly, appropriate breathing induces the breather into a state of increased relaxation. This is very important as tensed muscles react to pain much differently than do relaxed ones. Tense up, folks, and it hurts more. Relax and you can deal with pain much more effectively.

The other source for this knowledge comes from the years that I studied and practiced Transcendental Meditation. Yogis routinely teach their students breathing exercises that will first cause them to relax (hence the connection to La Maze) and then to move into an altered state. We may not use the term "altered state" very often, but it is simply another name for subspace. Ironically we don't really need those whips, paddles, and floggers to get where we want to go. Using impact play, though, does seem to be an easier way to get there. It is, after all, easier to get beaten into subspace than it is to learn how to meditate effectively. My advice, for what it's worth, is to learn and use both techniques simultaneously.

In their book, **The ManTantra Letters**, authors Victor Bliss and Nathan James discuss two breathing techniques between the partners. You can find similar techniques discussed in various sex manuals as well, and I strongly encourage partners to learn and apply them. They are both relatively simple. In the first case, the partners align the pace of their breathing; that is, they inhale and exhale simultaneously, thereby bringing their breathing into harmony and eventually their whole bodies into that state. Only one of the partners needs to be consciously aware of the other's pace and adapt to it, though it is helpful if they both knowingly cooperate with one another.

The second method is to breathe alternatively, the one partner inhaling as the other exhales, specifically inhaling the breath that the partner is exhaling. Our lungs use only a portion of the oxygen we inhale so there is plenty left over for the other partner. Besides, there's always a lot more air available during this technique as the breaths are not part of a closed system. Accompanying these breaths with the visualization of the exchange of energy, such as in the form of love, power, or light, greatly increases the effect. As a master, for instance, I imagine my giving to and taking breath from my slave. Lovers, friends, and various other kinds of partners can imagine sharing in terms that they find appropriate as well.

So there you have it. And you thought that breathing was just something we did. Well, we certainly do that, but the opportunity here is to do it better.

What then are the proper breathing techniques? Let me suggest that a simple search on Google using the terms "breathing techniques" (include the quotation marks) will answer that question quite well. I will, however, recount some ideas here. First off, it is important to become conscious of your breathing pattern. You can't change it unless you think about changing it. Rather than simply letting breathing be an automatic function, let your mind guide your breathing. That in itself will improve your breathing.

That said, then, practice your breathing in this way. Lie in a comfortable position wearing loose clothing. Be comfortable when you practice and then you can apply what you learn in most any situation.

Remember, too, that this exercise should be done slowly and in a relaxed fashion. If you have to force this breathing then you are doing it incorrectly. If you get dizzy, slow down or stop altogether until the dizziness passes.

It is helpful, too, if you remove any distractions and the environment is comfortable to you, i.e., the right temperature, quiet, and not so bright as to be distracting. Sounds like a good description for a dungeon to me.

Exhale. Now inhale from your stomach, then your chest, and finally your shoulders, slowly and gently pulling in lots of air. Slow and gentle are important here. The movement itself should be continuous and relaxed, as if you are slowly pouring a bottle of beer into a glass, or a fine wine if you prefer. You will fill your lungs from the "bottom up." Hold the breath in your expanded lungs for a short period and then exhale deeply and slowly. The idea is to fill them completely and empty them completely (though completely is only figurative here as you can't empty out all the air). Breathe like this for as long as you like. You are cleansing your lungs and refreshing your whole body. Relax and enjoy.

A Good Flogging

September 16, 2005

In September of 2005, Matthew, Patrick, and I had the pleasure of attending Inferno, Chicago Hellfire Club's annual anniversary celebration and get-away. A new adventure for Matt; he took it all in stride.

On Saturday night of the event, I mummified a first-time attendee and when that scene was over I turned my attention to Matt. I'm not much for paying a great amount of attention to my slaves when there's fresh meat to be played with, but I thought that Patrick was right in suggesting that I give Matt the "good flogging" he desired.

So I gathered up my floggers and a few restraints and we headed to a secluded St. Andrew's cross. One of the nice things about Inferno (and there are many) is that the protected and enclosed yards of the site give ample opportunity to play under the open sky. The weather cooperated exceptionally well as the temperature allowed full nudity and the clear sky gave a beautiful view of the stars. I fastened my slave to the cross, leaving his legs free and his arms bound low. With him in that position I would have to pay less attention to his hands, since circulation would not become a problem.

I'm usually too lazy to give a good flogging but even tyrants like myself have to keep their slaves happy lest one turn into a Spartacus and the rest follow his or her rebellious lead.

While I used a loose string flogger to warm up his back, we began to adjust to the intimacy, quiet, and pleasure of the scene to follow. I'm of the opinion that flogging, as most other scenes I create, is best accompanied by lots of skin-to-skin contact. That noted, you'll have to envision frequent pauses in our play as I rub his back, chest, neck, thighs, ass, and genitals to my heart's content. Occasionally I sneak in a kiss. There is full body contact as I lean myself against him, rubbing my cock into the crack of his ass. I pull on the chain around his neck and remind him that he is my property, my toy to play with as I please.

I might add some slaps of my hand to his back, tits, or cock and balls. At other times, I might scratch his back, adding even more color to the light pink that is beginning to show as a result of the flogger. In due time I'll progress through my collection of multi-tailed whips, using them in the order from easiest brusher to moderate thumper to severe stinger. Good flogging, after all, proceeds with a determined and growing intensity.

I watch for signs of strain, pushing Matt ever so slightly past his limits and then pausing so he can relax, letting the pain dissipate in the endorphin flow that begins to carry him to pleasure. So the string flogger gives way to an easier thudder as I pick a different patch of skin as my target. Later on I will require him to count the strokes.

Variety is also part of what I'm doing, as I hit different areas with varying intensity, sometimes right to left, sometimes left to right; now horizontally, then vertically. Once I can tell he is well-warmed and handling the pain without a problem, I'll flog for longer period of times. Since my slaves are experienced with me, I know that I can apply 100 strokes without too much of a problem. Later I'll aim for 200 in a row.

His back is quite pink now and there are a few marks making themselves known. My finger nails scratch his back more forcefully. I loosen him from the cross and turn him around so I can passionately kiss him on the lips while I dig my fingers into his scrotal sac, squeezing his nuts. He writhes in pain as I French kiss him.

I pull him away from the cross, turn him around and make him kneel. I slip between his face and the cross and order him to suck my cock. He might as well make me feel good as I wait for his body to grow accustomed to the pain.

With my hard shaft in full salute, I refasten him to the cross. This time his arms are raised high so that he has less wiggle room. I pick up a quirt that ends in two tails. It hurts and leaves nice red streaks. It is a bit hard to control, though, so I don't use it for very long. In a few minutes I put it down and pick up a lovely paint stirrer from Home Depot. The light, inch-wide wood will beat incessantly (or so it seems) on his shoulder blade, raising a crimson patch of skin. I am trying for black and blue but know that I may not get there.

Matt sobs some, a pleasant and hoped-for reaction that increases the stiffness of my prick. I am, after all, a sadist. He says "Stop" and I ignore him. He is a slave and my slaves have no right to say stop. Well, more correctly, they can say whatever they want, but I don't have to listen to them. Lest I get branded as an unsafe top, let me also add that even if they have no right to say stop, I have a responsibility not to injure them in any way, including psychologically. Safety is, even when I am sadistically aroused, an important consideration.

I only go a few slaps past the first stop, enough to make my point but not enough to ruin the scene. I loosen him again, move him backwards, lean against the cross, and tell him to suck. He lunges at my dick. I put my hands behind my head as it's his turn to do some work. He reaches up and amuses my tits with his hands while his lips and tongue give pleasure to my raging hard-on.

In reverie I look up and see the stars, hear the chirping night critters, and feel his warm wet slave mouth excite me. We will go on like this for an extended time: suck a little, flog a little, suck some more, flog some more. In the meantime I consider my next step.

I lean over and pick up a crop. There's no reason not to have him suck while I continue to beat him. Yes I am a greedy, demanding and horny bastard. Eventually I begin to think about shooting my load and how that might best happen. For his part, Matt is showing signs of real pleasure and a bit of fatigue. It's time to head up to our room, flop on the bed and consummate the night.

In the next few days, Matt will tell me more than once how good it was. Certainly, that's the way it's supposed to be. Floggings, after all, are meant to be good.

Adapting to Pain

July 15, 1997

One of the main impediments to developing an involvement in SM is the fear of pain. Fascinated as we are by the sensational, our literature, our gossip, our news, and our fantasies are more often filled with the exciting, the bizarre, and the difficult. After all, how often does the front page headline blare "Nice things happened today," or "Editors refuse to print stories of massacres, murders, and mayhem"?

So it's no surprise that the world associates leather sex with pain, whips, paddles, and sadism. I'm not saying that we don't deserve the association, merely noting that it's only one among many possible associations. How about associating leather sex with trust, with bonding, with friendship, with fun? Somehow I don't think that would make for hot news or good gossip.

It wasn't surprising that I once read the following on an Internet newsgroup:

"I am a 45-year-old white American male living in Asia who hopes to soon become the slave of an Asian Master. I truly love this master, and wish to be completely submissive and obedient to him. Yet, I fear the relationship because my possible master is sadistic. Is there any way that I can prepare for this? I spent two years in household slavery, but this part is new for me. Any suggestions will be greatly appreciated. I have learned so much from all the regulars on the newsgroup gl-subs. Thanks, Roy"

Some of the more experienced regulars on the list have given me permission to quote their answers.

"Well, this worked for me. Explain that you are very new to that aspect of slavery. Sadism can be fun and the pain that your potential master will give is his gift to you. It can take you on some very interesting rides. I think that you shouldn't fight the pain. If you do, it will not be fun. Anyway, as I always say to my friends COMMUNICATE!!! Nowhere has anyone said that you can't tell a potential master where you are and what you have done in the past. In fact, it helps as far as his decisions in your training and how he or she will treat you. Give communication a chance. [signed] Boy"

I remember that when Patrick first came to me I asked

him if he were a masochist. His rather prompt reply was that he wasn't. That remark, of course, didn't stop me from gifting him with a warm butt or sore back whenever my sadistic feelings led me to do so.

Patrick accepted the pain as a way to give me pleasure. Over the course of the first few months of our relationship, I gave him the spankings, whippings, and pinchings I wanted. I find the infliction of pain to be a tremendous turn-on. Though he didn't feel the same way, he was turned on by the act of obedience and of knowing that he was giving me pleasure.

I'm generally careful to gauge the severity of my sadism and to provide the necessary support and instruction the would-be masochist needs in order to successfully undergo the event. That is the way the vast majority of tops are. We help our bottoms past their limits so that both of us get what we want.

A woman from San Francisco named Teramis offered her view:

> When I was new to the scene I used to think I was a very light masochist. I was, I suppose, because mentally the thought of much pain was distinctly not a turn on. I would see people get caned bloody, for instance, and say, 'Wow, interesting. But not for me.'
>
> Eventually, however, I came to a place where, if I took pain in the process of submitting to my dominant's will, it became an incredible turn-on, because doing so was such an exercise of her control over me, and that (the control issue) was the actual erotic crux of the event for me. To be made to hurt because it pleases her.... that was what got me mentally accustomed to the concept that I could withstand great pain. And it became erotic in the process. Now I am a pretty heavy masochist and enjoy certain sensations for the pain alone, though it is always much more charged and erotic when I am being 'dommed' into it.
>
> The point to this rambling is that if you are more of a submissive than a bottom, you may not be into sensation (pain) play, and that is not an unusual attitude at all amongst submissives. However, you may very well find that if you are doing it to please your dom, pain becomes something transcendent of mere sensation.
>
> A last thought --- my biggest breakthroughs in becoming a heavy masochist happened in no-safeword[1] play, wherein I was forced to simply resign myself and surrender completely to whatever my Owner wanted to do to me, since I had no out and no recourse but to endure. When you can no longer fight it or shy away from it, you must simply go through it. It makes sensation play a very

---

1 It 's important to remind my readers that Teramis is writing about a scene with a trusted partner with whom she shares a long-term relationship. This fact greatly alters the need for a safeword.

different thing, than when you have the ability to halt stuff that you 'think' is over your limit. --- Teramis

Over the course of time, then, both Teramis and Patrick had similar experiences. First they learned to accept and then to enjoy the pain.

Any experienced masochist will tell you that "Resistance is futile." It is accepting and surrendering to the pain that indeed makes the pain "go away," to be replaced by euphoria that makes masochism attractive and pleasurable.

Secondly, relationship factors have a very high level of importance. What Teramis would accept from her owner she probably wouldn't take from some guy across the street. I may get to beat the Hell out of Patrick without the slightest complaint on his part, but I know that a stranger would not be allowed to get away with it.

Once again I have to come to the conclusion that the leather lifestyle works because of the close bonds that we build with each other. The problem described by the novice with the Asian Master is solved by surrender, by practice, and by the intensity of the relationship.

My former lover Michael, who was a masochist, and a good one at that, was quick to say that it's not so much how the beating is given as by whom. Two identical inflictions of pain, for instance, will be felt as significantly different depending upon who is administering them.

There's nothing new about that line. Intensity in a leather relationship is always determined by the depth of trust that is built between the partners. Therein lies the secret of dealing with pain. If you can "let go" you will move through it much more easily and quickly. Doing so, of course demands that you want to and that you can trust the person making you "deal" with it. Given those two qualifications, there's not as much pain as one might fear.

In fact, as Boy said, "It can take you on some very interesting rides."

The Other End of the Flogger

December, 1997

It takes two to tango," my Mom always said, and that certainly applies to a good flogging session. Oh, the Franciscans may do it alone, but we Leather folk prefer to make it a communal event.

When Steve so expertly applied his floggers to Al's bare back at a Master and slave Training Seminar, we all made sure we paid attention. It was a sight to behold.

It's easy to note that Steve knows what he's doing. Likewise the same must be said of his slave Al. Just as my essay on flogging had all sorts of advice for tops, there are suggestions for bottoms as well.

As you've read here many times before, all SM scenes demand a certain level of trust that must escalate if the intensity of the scene is to rise. Flogging, therefore, demands great mutual trust. If it isn't present then settle for something less or nothing at all. The first rule for the bottom, then, is if you can't trust your top, don't be his bottom.

There's always time to get to know him or her better and have the scene later.

Good tops have to know how to "read" their bottoms, how to recognize signals that contain important information. Communication is a two-way street. It is imperative that the bottom communicate before and during the session.

What are some of the ways you can do that?

Speak up. An inability to say what you feel is the first warning sign that something is wrong. Ask your questions. Warn of dangers. Inform your top of your physical conditions, especially of any medical limitations. Answer your top's questions honestly. Forewarned is best armed.

The last paragraph is meant to be done before the flogging (or any other SM for that matter) begins, but it does not and should not stop there. Speak up during the flogging if need be as well. This is no time to think that "Silence is golden."

The third piece of advice is to continue to communicate throughout the scene. The best way to do that is to emote. The idea that one should "tough it out" in silence is rather self-defeating for a number of reasons.

We sadists like to hear you yell and scream. It is that re-action that gets our juices flowing. Venting your pain with noise will make the pain easier to take and will help release the energy aroused by the beating.

I want to make it clear that I'm not talking about making noise for the mere satisfaction of making noise, to prove some point or impress someone. When I use the word "emote," I am writing about an honest expression of one's feelings.

In fact emoting is much more than yelling and scream-ing. Chances are that if it's only that, then there is more than a bit of pretense involved, and that defeats good communication. No, emoting includes wriggling, writhing, and crying — any reac-tion that the natural body wants to make to what goes on when the whip meets the skin.

Yes, there are moments when toughing it out and taking it have meaning, but to purposefully conceal what you are really feeling will soon vanquish any possibility of a good scene.

If the top has all those guidelines for wielding the whip, the bottom has fewer, but ones that are just as important. I hate to boil the next instruction down to one word, but it is the best advice I can give: relax. Having come to the conclusion that you want to be flogged and that you can honestly trust the person who's going to do it, then relax and let them do their job. Tenseness is only go-ing to make matters worse. The best advice about relaxing comes from the books on natural childbirth. I won't go into all the relevant techniques here but there are three that are important --- breath control, muscle control, and visualization.

Correct breathing is probably the single most important way to sustain the pain. Simply put, breathe slowly and deeply and keep on doing it. Quick shallow breaths will lead to hyper-ventilation, though at times the natural birth-ers will suggest that technique as well.

Deep breaths will help you relax, especially when coupled with the visualization that the pain is being released as you ex-hale. As the air enters, feel your chest enlarge and think about the air radiating throughout your body, bringing healthy, healing, and cleansing oxygen to your system. As you physically expand on the intake, see yourself expanding into the universe.

During the exhalation part of the breath, imagine that the out-going air carries with it impurities, pain, and energy. You are becoming a conduit and the pain flows quickly and easily through you as each and every breath leaves your body.

Becoming tense is a very natural reaction to being whipped. We want to recoil from pain, and the action of our mus-cles is to tighten up. Just as we can control our muscles and make them tighten, so too can we make them relax. It's certainly not as easy a proposition, but it can be done if we take time to think about it and do it. Tenseness in our muscles is going to increase the feeling of pain. Conversely, relaxing is going to make the pain a great deal easier to take.

This is why I write so seriously about bondage. Those restraints allow you to relax. One of their purposes is to give you the freedom to "go limp." They will hold you so you can relax without fear of collapsing.

They also allow you to struggle without flailing, thereby getting the effect of the muscular reaction without any of the danger of moving into the wrong position at the wrong time. Go ahead and emote by moving, and then remember to relax. You'll always want to remember to relax, and a good top will help you do that.

Tops will caress, kiss, and soothe with touch and words. Most importantly they should remind you to relax and to breathe. After all, you're in this together.

Visualization is a rather personal event so you'll have to come up with ideas that fit your style and have the positive effects we're seeking. Visualization is using your imagination to create mind-pictures of events that illustrate what you want to happen. I often use the imagery of light. For me, SM is fundamentally a sharing of power, of energy if you will. I visualize sharing as a light beam that moves from me to my partner and back again.

Similarly I "see" the pain hit me and I "see" my body change the pain into light. I then imagine the light radiating safely and easily into the universe. I suppose you could say that I visualize myself as a light bulb; the pain is the electric current, and when the current passes through me I light up. That, of course, is the whole purpose of the flogging. For me, flogging in and of itself isn't the end, it is the means to an end, namely the state of relaxation, of pleasure, of bliss that will come when both of us are sated.

It is the afterglow that makes all of SM, and especially the more sadistic practices such as whipping and paddling, a reasonable and desirable event. Until you experience the afterglow, none of this makes much sense, really. Done well, to be on the receiving end of whip is a cathartic, liberating, and exhilarating experience. Come on over, my floggers are ready.

Cleaning Out

February 15, 1998

When a reader recently asked me about the dangers associated with enemas, I did what I advise all my readers to do: Ask your doctor.

Since coming to Chicago I have been blessed with one of the best doctors in the world. At least that's my opinion of him. He is supportive, interested, and medically astute. He's also very handsome. Sometimes I want to get another doctor just so I can fool around with this one. Every time I tell him that, though, he reminds me that he is happily married. "No problem," I say. "I'll have sex with both of you." Needless to say, it does me no good.

His advice, on the other hand, is quite valuable so I'm going to let the doctor[1] speak first:

"There really isn't anything wrong with using enemas per se, but it depends on what kind of enema one is using. Typically an enema is used for two purposes: to stimulate the colon if one is constipated or to cleanse the colon before a medical procedure. Obviously, we're not talking about those situations. As you can imagine, very little has been written about the non-medical use of enemas in the medical literature.

"The most frequent problem we encounter is the person who uses enemas chronically for constipation. Chronic use can cause a condition called 'melanosis coli.' On examination, the colon has a blackish pigmentation. This isn't dangerous, but a person can become 'dependent' on enemas. If one uses an enema that is hypotonic [having an osmotic pressure lower than that of an isotonic substance] with respect to the blood, too much fluid may be absorbed into the circulatory system, causing fluid overload in a person with impaired heart, liver or kidney function. A hypertonic solution can cause the reverse--dehydration. If various chemicals are added to the enema, they can be absorbed, possibly causing physical harm. So it depends what is in the enema.

"Some people use 'herbal' enemas, which are probably safe, as long as the amount used is relatively low. A gallon seems like a high quantity to me. Most enemas on the shelves of pharma-

---

1 And here again you ought to consult with your doctor, especially if my doctor's vocabulary in this essay is as difficult for you as it was for me.

cies are much smaller amounts.

"Another possible problem is rupture of the colon if the colon is filled too quickly--an obviously dangerous situation.

"I don't think that anyone should use wine or catnip in enemas or anything weird, for that matter. In the old days before IVs were invented, doctors used to hydrate people with enemas, which worked fairly well. The colon is very absorbent. I would recommend only those solutions that approximate in composition the blood plasma--and in limited quantities. The stuff you get over the counter is fairly benign, but you only should use one or two bottles during a 'session.'

"The best advice is to follow the golden rule: anything in moderation is probably ok."

Thank you, doctor!

The question my reader posed had to do with the danger of using too much solution and thereby causing pain. Obviously, if the doc's guidelines are followed, there won't be pain. On the other hand, some of us like to inflict pain and doing so might be part of the "gig." Enemas or cleaning out is sometimes called douching, though the last time I used that term it was confused with the female variation of the same process. Let's make it clear. I'm talking about putting fluids into the rectum via the anus. There are two sex-related reasons for doing this: the first is as preparation for anal play, the second is as part of anal play itself.

A lot of guys are concerned that they "clean out" before receptive anal sex. My fisting friends, of course, will tell you that doing so is very important. Most people don't want to put their hand into an ass and come out with a fist full of shit. Therefore cleaning before you play is seen as mandatory. I'm not a purist in that regard but I do advise a quick trip to the potty for anyone who thinks they're going to take anyone or anything up their ass.

The simplest way to administer an enema is to use one or two "Fleets." No household should be without them! You buy them at the drug store, usually in packages of two, use them once, and throw them away. Since they come with a full set of instructions, I'll let you read that for yourself. Use the generic kind as they're cheaper and just as good.

I, of course, was raised on the old-fashioned water bottle, hose, and nozzle. My grandmother thought an enema would cure anything! I have since come to prefer the rubber squeeze bulb variety, but both work rather well.

The precautions that the doctor didn't mention are fairly obvious. The liquid needs to be approximately body temperature. Too hot or too cold is too dangerous. The equipment and the fluids need to be clean and sterile. A bit of water soluble lubricant on the nozzle of the enema bag helps as well.

Fill yourself, or your partner, slowly, stopping frequently to allow your muscles to adjust to the fluid. Once you have enough inside, you only need wait a few minutes before you will be ready to evacuate. I almost sound like a doctor, don't I?

My first experiences with erotic enemas took place in Indianapolis, during the summer of my "coming out." I had met a guy at the baths who took me home. In the following weeks we became good friends. He was a nurse and into ass play.

He, his partner, and their friends used to mix all sorts of things into the water they used for enemas. On the top of the list was wine, quickly followed by catnip tea. They were careful to use such ingredients in diluted form. As Doc would say, "Be careful and be moderate."

One time a guy wanted to fist me and I was willing to try. Before he came over I gave myself an enema and added some vodka to the warm water. I figured it would help relax me. Unfortunately, by the time he got there I was too drunk to be of any good! Live and learn. Right?

Though I have tended to get lazy in my old age, I used to routinely give enemas to the bottoms who came over to play. Not only can it be erotic in itself, I find it a dominating kind of thing. I think of it as making the ass mine.

Once the cavity is filled with warm water, it can be a very nice experience to fuck in it. Try it, you'll like it. Every thrust provokes a slosh, if you know what I mean.

Of course all this is going to take preparation and the right kind of equipment. I reserve this kind of play for the bathroom and have lots of old towels lying around. You'll want to be sure you do the same.

More on Ass Play

March 12, 1998

That essay on enemas makes a suitable entrée into this topic: Fucking. Since most people prefer to fuck a clean ass, cleansing is certainly an appropriate preparation.

Of course I need to be quick to point out that humans have more than one orifice into which a dick may be put. The word fucking, then, might well be preceded by the word face, ass, or cunt. For this essay, I'm going to write about the last two, as face fucking is much more about sucking.

Unfortunately, intercourse isn't as easy as society pretends. I say pretends because one would think that the details of an event as important as sex would be well taught to our children. Instead we leave it to experimentation and chance, with perhaps a library book, a friend, or a porno flick thrown in for good measure. What we don't do with any of that is pass on the techniques that make fucking satisfying.

Maybe it shows that I've always been a little slow on the uptake, but I was married for more than three days before my bride and I were able to consummate our wedding. Whoever said that getting laid came naturally wasn't thinking of us!

Years later, I was well into my own coming-out process when I first fucked my friend Mike. At the time he was a trick I had picked up at a local bar. I remember him wanting to be fucked early that Sunday morning. I obliged, and was astounded to see that he really liked having a cock (my cock) up his ass.

I, of course, didn't try the same feat with my anus until a good three years later. And yes, it hurt the first time. And yes, sometimes it still hurts.

Fucking doesn't have to hurt, of course. Done right it can be downright satisfying for both partners. Done right means with ample preparation and due care.

Preparation is more than just foreplay. Like any muscle group, both the anus and the vagina need to be appropriately loosened in order for a cock (or a dildo) to fit in comfortably. Practicing with a small dildo and working up to larger sizes is part of the preparation.

Due care is foreplay. Due care is a slow speed, the right position, gentleness, lubrication, condoms, and trust. Fucking, after all, isn't meant to be rape. It's meant to be intimacy.

No one ever (except in utero) comes as close to another person as when he (or she) is inside the other, or conversely as when he or she has the other person inside them. The receptive part can squeeze and caress the inserted member. For its part the inserter can stroke and poke the insertee in wonderfully sensuous ways. The result is pleasure.

For the top, the pleasure often leads to orgasm. Surprisingly, many bottoms don't come when being fucked, but do get significant enjoyment and satisfaction from the activity. For those comfortable and knowledgeable in the techniques of love-making (another euphemism for fucking), orgasm remains the end (as in purpose) of sex but the act of sex is widely regarded as much greater than the orgasm itself.

In fact for many folk, orgasm is overshadowed by all the pleasures derived before.

In light of AIDS, many partners refrain from orgasm during fucking. Even though they go at it with a high margin of safety by using condoms and a virucidal lubricant, they withdraw prior to orgasm and have their ejaculation outside of their partner's body. I admit that my writing takes a definitive male predilection in these lines so I'll have to ask my female readers to use their imaginations when it comes to their being "insertive". That poses no more problem, I'm sure, than it does for male readers to be "receptive."

The whole point of fucking is, after all, intimacy and we should and can be creative in ways to accomplish that goal. The physical inclusion of one's member in another's body is only one way that fucking accomplishes its objective. The bonds of unity in SM fucking (i.e., safe, sane, and consensual) are formed with one's emotions as well as one's flesh and blood.

We in the Western World don't often consider the energies of our ethereal bodies. Those of the East, particularly those who practice Yoga, Tantra, or any of those related Buddhist, Vedic, and Hindu philosophies, have much to teach us in this area. Suffice it to say that there is more to fucking than just fucking.

What has always attracted me to leather is the willingness of its adherents to explore, experiment, and actually devote time, energy, and thought to sex and sexual pleasure.

I'm not advocating the quick fuck that turns a trick into an object, a "fucker" into no more than a human dildo, though there are certainly enough reasons to have a quickie now and again. In the early days of several of my relationships it was not uncommon to do it on the couch during a half hour lunch break.

But serious fucking, like anything else worth doing, takes time. Develop your technique, prepare the space, go at it slowly, build to climax. The operative word here is "slowly". Make fucking playful, while keeping it deliberate and varied. I was going to add the word "tender", then thought about fucking being rough, and finally realized that the best word is "varied", since both tender and rough have their place in intimacy.

There are times for ramming one's rod or riding an erect cock as if it were a wildly rocking horse, but the best fucks are crafted with a gradual rise toward climax. Some even advocate that one develop the ability to have an orgasm without ejaculation so that multiple orgasms become possible in a shorter period of time.

Our culture has a fundamental prejudice against sex. I've railed enough against that premise already. Americans, and probably most of the societies on this planet, are embarrassed and ashamed about fucking. Hence the lack of available instruction (not to mention unwanted pregnancy and sexual dysfunction).
I mentioned to a friend that I was writing about fucking and he said "Why? What's to learn?"

Our attitudes about sex as "being private" and "being dirty" are misguided. We choose to pretend that satisfactory sex is merely instinctual, needs no prompting, and is best gotten over with as soon as possible. In my adolescence, intercourse was discussed in terms of "marital obligations, procreation, and the alleviation of concupiscence."

Those are hardly terms that engender pleasure. Fucking is about pleasure. Make that pleasure with care, responsibility, and intimacy. Make it safe fucking, but make it fun.

Learn how to fuck -- and how to get fucked. Read, watch, discuss. Approach fucking as a blessing. The world would be a better place if we did.

Anal Intercourse

March 09, 1997

When Joe (not his real name) once wrote asking me to fuck him, his letter hit a friendly, erotic spot in me. I replied in the affirmative and said "Come on over for dinner and we'll see what happens." If dinner goes well, we'll probably make it to the bedroom, but I prefer to start with no promises and no expectations.

That's part of the attitude I've developed over the years. Having met thousands of men and had hundreds of dates, I've learned to stay flexible, non-judgmental, and easy-going. I've done my best to remove feelings of "should" or "have to." One day, one step at a time.

Joe's letter demonstrates the simple fact that there's little in sex that comes naturally. I suppose that instinct teaches us the basics, but the finer movements, the greater pleasure, only comes with practice and information.

"The reason I'm writing, by the way," Joe writes, "is believe it or not I've never really been completely satisfied sexually. All I want is vanilla sex with someone fucking me and making me feel good as I hope to make that person feel good. I know that I would be tight therefore making it painful but once I get into it, I know I would really enjoy it."

Joe isn't in the minority when it comes to sex. Most people could have better sex, and have it more often, if they only knew how. Successful sex is a combination of attitude, technique, preparation, and emotion.

I'm not going to include all of Joe's letter in this column, but the paragraph I did quote gives an insight into what I mean. Joe wants his sex to be mutually enjoyable. That's important. That's part of the right attitude.

Later on he writes "I want to be with someone who knows what he's doing, who has experience." Not a bad idea either. Joe recognizes that the best sex comes from knowing how to do it and that the knowledge must be learned. Having a mentor for that learning process is an idea whose time has come. Believe me, dating a man with experience has more going for it than just a free dinner.

I'm not about to deny that Joe's right about the pain part, either. Sometimes getting fucked hurts. Sometimes getting fucked hurts real good. Here again, attitude, preparation, and technique can mitigate the pain and increase the pleasure. Let me take those thoughts one at a time.

You've probably read me enough that I need not dwell on what's the right attitude. Relax. Let go of expectations. You don't have to get fucked. You don't have to fuck someone else. If you're doing it, whatever it is, because of a sense of obligation or necessity, then you need to analyze your true feelings and adjust your actions accordingly. Sexual activity should never be a matter of must. When it is, you open yourself up to lots of disappointment.

I know. Ask Patrick. There are plenty of nights when one or the other of us isn't up to doing something. More than once I've tried to fuck him and have been unsuccessful. Dicks have minds of their own. So dispel the pressure to perform and rid yourself of expectations about what's going to happen. Go with the flow of the moment.

That doesn't mean one shouldn't be prepared. Have a good supply of condoms handy, as well as water soluble lubricant, latex gloves, and clean and sterile small-to-medium sized dildoes. Tops should trim their fingernails and bottoms should give themselves an enema.

There's more to preparations than that, too. Notice that I invited Joe to dinner. I've met him once (that's why he felt able to write me) but quality time spent before we "hit the sack" is not only a good idea, but a big part of the process. Each of us has to be comfortable with one another, before anything really enjoyable is going to happen.

We won't rush to fuck, either. Foreplay is important. Explore each other slowly and carefully. Kissing, disrobing each other, feeling under each other's clothes, and simply cuddling gets the action pointed in the right direction.

Be careful to create a mood with music, lighting, the right temperature, and an appropriate place to do what you're going to do. Vanilla sex, for instance, is probably more easily done on a bed than in a sling. Leather sex, on the other hand, is hotter in a dungeon than on a couch. In any case, though, you'll have to work with what's available.

So you've gotten each other hot and bothered. Now's the time for serious preparation for entry. Put on a glove, coat your fingers liberally with lube, squirt a good portion of it on the anus, and begin to tickle his or her rosebud. Pace yourself and do a lot of teasing. Rub your fingers in a circular motion around the hole. Poke into it slowly and, at first, only superficially. At the same time, arouse your partner with kisses, sexy talk, and/or your other hand.

Sucking or stroking his cock, for instance, as you play with

64 his anus, will make his ass respond more quickly to your intentions. As your partner's anus relaxes, you'll be able to do more and get more. A little deeper, a little wider, always making sure that there's plenty of lube on the right places.

Your partner, meanwhile, will want to reciprocate: he or she should forget about his or her ass and concentrate on arousing and satisfying you. As Mom says, "It takes two to tangle [sic]."

Having gotten this far, use a small dildo to play with the hole. The sphincter muscles around the anus can open quite wide, but only as they get used to being spread. Once again, slow is what gets the job done. We're not rapists here. We're looking for mutual satisfaction.

Dildoes are helpful beforehand, too. There's no reason that a bottom can't "practice" getting fucked at home, at his own pace, graduating to larger and larger dildoes as practice makes entry easier.

I hope you get the idea. In all of this, pause frequently, be cuddly, and remember that this is supposed to be fun, not work. If it feels like work, you're going at it too fast and too hard.

By now your stiff cock, covered with a condom and lubricated well, ought to be ready to put where the sun doesn't shine. This is the painful moment that Joe fears. It doesn't have to be, of course. For starters, the top can simply lie on his back, stroke his dick into a good stiff heat, and let the bottom sit on it. This allows the bottom to control the entry and helps to alleviate a goodly amount of pain.

To do this, straddle the top and rub your anus over his prick. Tease yourself and his cock. Play with his tits while he strokes your cock. For the third time, there's no need to rush. When your hole is hungry enough, take his cock in your hand and begin to stick into yourself. It helps to alternate squeezing your sphincter muscles open and closed. You'll also have an easier time of getting it in if you push out, as if you're taking a dump.

Once the prick's head gets past the first set of muscles you'll find the going gets a hell of a lot easier. After all, even slightly larger penises aren't any bigger than a healthy crap. If the channel is large enough for something to come out, it's large enough for something to go in.

Once it's in, stop. Don't move. Take a moment to let the cock stay inside you as you get used to its being there. If there is more pain than you like, ease up a bit, but don't let it out. The pain will subside fairly quickly and you can then sit on the cock more fully. In no time at all your rose bud will be rubbing pubic hair. It also helps for you to grab each of your ass cheeks and spread them so that you can better encase the cock.

Now's the time for both of you to enjoy it. The fucker can make slow, long thrusting movements, while the fuckee can "suck" the dick with his sphincter, squeezing it and releasing it. You may want to maneuver into other positions. It can be done if you move slowly. Or you may want to let him slip out so he can re-enter from above, or the back, or however.

The best fucks, as with any kind of sex, are mutually pleasurable because each partner is doing his or her best to arouse and satisfy the other. If you think you'll get a good fuck by just lying there, you're wrong. Simply put, concentrate on pleasuring the other and you'll both have a grand time.

Flesh

November 21, 2004

My friend Larry complained that my writing is "too political" and that I needed to write on some hot and steamy topic for a change. He's right, of course, because when our kink is too cerebral, too political, or too sanitized, it stops being fun. Fun is, after all, the best reason to be doing what we're doing. I've noticed recently that I take great pleasure in flesh so I hope you get some fun out of this column.

I often start a sexual encounter with Patrick by having him lie next to me on my bed to cuddle and talk. The prelude to what it is that we do, for him and me, is pretty vanilla as we quietly and intimately talk about the day, the news, the weather, or whatever might hit our fancy. From there I stretch out my arm and signal for him to cozy up to me in a warm embrace.

He, as is usual, is naked. I most often have my shirt off but leave my pants and socks on, as it's his job to strip me when I'm ready. In the meantime he nestles his head against my shoulder and often puts his leg atop mine so it is touching my crotch. I gently stroke his chest or head, perhaps caress his face, play with his tits, or stroke his beautiful cock.

I love touching him. I mean I really love touching him.

There is an incredible variety to his flesh, and each part of his body offers a different sensation. His chest is usually shaved, though at times there is a feeling of stubble, if it's been a few days. His back is shaved less often, as it gets done only when he asks a friend or a visiting slave to shave it for him. Hair isn't usually a problem, though, as he is mostly bald and what hair he has is silky and short.

Patrick complains that I am too predictable in bed these days and I probably am. After nine years of playing together he surely knows me well enough to know my habits, routines, and favorite moves, just as I know what turns him on and what he really only tolerates. He has learned to grin and bear it, though I hope that I can say that I have learned how to keep him happy as well.

My prick keeps him happy so it's not too long before I tire of cuddling and tell him to suck my dick. I'm much more adventuresome when I'm sexually aroused and I strongly believe that it is the duty of the slave to arouse the master. So I tell him to get to it --- and he does.

In that we are compatible. Sucking my cock is his number one favorite thing and it ranks highest on my list as well. So he scoots down the bed, I spread my legs and he feasts on "Master Cock." It is a grand position to be in. His face is in my crotch, his lips sink down my male shaft to kiss my pubic hairs and press his mouth against my pubic bone. His hands automatically reach up to brush my tits.

I adjust my legs on each side of his chest, feeling the warmth of his flesh against mine. I nuzzle my knees beneath him so that they squeeze his tits as well. In a few minutes I might break the action long enough to put tit clamps on him, as the cool of the metal and the warmth of his chest make a sensuous combination.

When we begin thusly, I am flat on my back, so his head, arms, and shoulders are most visible. It's here that I begin my first reverie into the beauty of flesh, as his shoulders are naturally smooth, his skin beautiful to touch. As I caress them, I feel the power of his muscles and the strength of his bones beneath my traveling hands.

Flesh touches flesh. I knead his flesh and squeeze the muscles they shelter. I run my fingers down his arms, across the back of his neck, shoving his hungry, wet, warm, mouth deeper onto my prick. I'll probably begin to get verbal here, but that is material for another column.

If I were still in elementary school, I'd be diagnosed with Attention Deficiency Disorder as I don't stay on any one thing for very long, much to Patrick's consternation. So in a few minutes, I stretch out my left arm, letting my hand reach over the side of the bed and snap my fingers. It's my signal for him to get up and put his testicles into the palm of my hand, where I can touch them and take ownership of them as is my slave-given right.

It is a different kind of flesh here, thicker, and textured with creases. His testicles present a pleasurable feeling as well, as they float inside the sack, slipping as best they can from my grasp, but caught nonetheless in the grip of my fingers.

There are so many places to touch and such a wide variety of sensations to feel. It's not just fingers that touch, either. My skin feels his, my dick enjoys his flesh, my tongue licks and tastes while my eyes behold and my nose catches his manly scents.

Soon I release his scrotum and move my fingers to the smooth, forbidden skin between his scrotum and his anus. This is mine as well and I love touching him there, squeezing the flesh and feeling the ring I had put there so that I could control him. I slip a finger into the ring and stretch the skin. In time I will move my fingers up to his anus, circling it with my fingertips.

Here is another sensation, preeminently smoother and, as my finger moves into the darkness of his asshole, I feel its moisture and its warmth. It is the power I have to break taboos that I enjoy. I can hear my mother say "Don't touch that. It's dirty," and I revel in the iconoclasm and the effrontery of it all.

There will be more of this later. Now his mouth sucks one of my tits, his hand plays with the other. I feel myself, stroking my spit-covered prick. I move up on the bed, resting against pillows and the headboard and send him back between my legs. Now I have the pleasurable view of his gorgeous ass. The two mounds of his flesh cheeks invite my eyes to view and my brain to figure out what comes next.

All that is to say, Larry, that when you're playing, remember to watch, to taste, to smell, and to touch. Make your BDSM a whole body event and have fun doing it.

A Short, But Important, Sentence

December 01, 2002

Like many submissives, my slave Patrick is a quiet person, not given to volunteering a great deal of information. It's natural for him to remain alone, involved in his own projects, attentive to my needs but often very inconspicuous. We agree that slaves should be "seen and not heard," to paraphrase my mother's dictum to my brother and me.

So I was pleasantly surprised one morning when he commented that "Play last night was fun, Sir." I wasn't so surprised that it was fun, as it most certainly was, but rather that he mentioned it to me. He is very sparse on the comments, to be sure, but that sentence was important.

Feedback, though, is really of the highest importance in what we do. Last night, for instance, I had been inspired by a recent porno movie to wrap Patrick in plastic wrap. I know that he enjoys bondage and the mummification shown in the movie was a real turn-on to me so I waited for the right time, namely when we had no reason to get up the next morning, and wrapped him in plastic, reinforcing stress areas with duct tape.

I get my enjoyment from bondage because it allows me full rein on his body without his squirming and yelling getting in my way. The wrap is a means to an end, his immobility, not an end in itself, though he would probably like it that way. So there he was with only his feet, mouth, and nose exposed as I lay him on the bed. Now it was time for seeing how effective my "lip training" had been, as I applied four clothespins to his mouth. In order to distract him from that pain, I carefully cut the wrap around his dick and added clothespins, first to his scrotum and then to his prick. Sadism is so much fun.

Anyway, to get back to the meat of this essay, you can see why Patrick's positive feedback is important. We're playing at a level of intensity that scares off most people, so knowing that he enjoys it is particularly important.

I know that some of you think that if he were a real slave, his opinion wouldn't matter. In that case I dare say you err. If partners, no matter how dominant/submissive their relationship, don't get tangible benefits from their mutual play, they are going to stop playing. It's as simple as that. The "I have no limits" crowd doesn't know what it is saying, as our bodies will react strongly when our instincts and our fears feel the need to protect us. Quite frankly it's much easier to stop sooner than later, because if you don't the blow-up will not be fun.

In the early stages of our SM experience, feedback is given through the use of safe words. Experienced players, on the other hand, often don't use safe words, as they develop a keen awareness of what works and what doesn't and have honed their instinct, their ESP, and their ability to read body language.

As Master Panman wrote in an issue of Collars Newsletter: "Is there such a thing as having no safe word? I don't use safe words but, then, My own eroticism is stimulated by knowing (visibly and audibly) that the slave hungers for what I am giving him and wants more. For Me the slave's demeanor is a safe word and has often times been more 'safe' than the slave wanted."

In spite of my use of instinct, ESP, and the reading of body language, it is a plain fact that neither masters nor slaves are mind readers. For that reason it is imperative that partners inform one another about their feelings, fears, thoughts, and desires. Once we begin to cease to communicate on meaningful levels, relationships fail, even if it takes years for us to discover that such has become the case.

Feedback during the event is certainly essential but so is the need to communicate in a more formal setting, where the accoutrements of whips and chains aren't a distraction. Patrick and I have a regular Sunday night "check in time" where we are both free to express our feelings and desires. It is a simple routine that most often indicates there is nothing to discuss, but at least we have made the time available.

Occasionally, of course, we do need to talk, even when we think we have said enough.

That was brought home to me one weekend. I think we were playing and I said something that now totally escapes me. Patrick then commented that he thought the demands I made during our sex/play were simply part of the play and had no real meaning out of that context. For months now (ten to be exact) I have been telling him I wanted more slavery, more obedience, more submission, and more control.

He had no idea that I meant it in the context of our total relationship. He naturally took that in the context of our BDSM and received it as hot talk in bed.

Though it was certainly that, I meant it as much more, as I had begun to become dissatisfied with non-sexual variables in our relationship, many over which neither of us has any control, such as when he gets home from work and which chores get done first, or at all. Even so, I had never said this outside of the bedroom so it was natural for him to take it in that context. His comment, that I only meant it as play, turned a light bulb on for me.

I made a mental note to speak to the situation in a non-threatening, non-sexual venue, when we could discuss what I wanted and what I meant. The next day I did so and it was then that the lights went on for Patrick as well, for now he knew how I felt and what I wanted, actions that resonated with his desires as well. Gags may have their place in our dungeons, but every once in a while you've got to take them off, share your thoughts, and listen as well.

Raunch: Read at Your Own Risk

August 22, 1994

More delicate readers may find this essay offensive. If that includes you, please don't read any further. I would also like to warn that the material included herein, for the sake of space, contains only scant advice concerning safety and health. The sharing of bodily fluids or of fecal matter poses serious risks. These risks can be minimized but you won't find those instructions here. Those risks are significant, though, and you should know them and avoid or minimize them before involving yourself in raunchy activities. Enough said; know how to play safely and do so.

Raunch comes in several different and disgusting varieties. It includes food, oil, grease, dirt and grime, spit and snot, sweat, urine, and last, but not least, shit, aka scat. You see, not all SM contains an element of pain. Humiliation and iconoclasm work well in this kind of scene, too.

I once went to an entertaining show at Fantasy '94 in Omaha, Nebraska which had a very funny skit. A guy comes to dinner bringing flowers and a box of candy. The host meets him at the door, whips him with the flowers, stuffs the candy onto his head and then shoves him into a rather large roasting pan. Once this feat is accomplished he bastes him with catsup, mustard, and chocolate sauce and stuffs croutons up his ass and down his mouth. The whole riotous scene was reminiscent of a seventh grade food fight.

I used to go swimming at an abandoned gravel quarry. Its remoteness made it conducive to nude bathing. One afternoon three of us discovered a huge pool of mud and immediately tromped into it, rubbing the black ooze over our bodies and throwing it at each other. Mud wrestling is another "leather" activity, but one where you probably won't want to wear leather. Similar scenes can take place with whipped cream, motor oil, Jell-o, and pudding.

Not all raunch is external to the human body. Golden showers, the spraying of a partner with piss right from one's cock or cunt, are much more popular and done much more frequently than more modest players admit. Taking excrement one step further, there are those who play in shit, either their own or someone else's. Perhaps lesser-used vehicles of raunch include snot and spit. I write "perhaps" because I don't know what the statistics might be, and anyway who's counting?

There are several directions this discussion can take. On the one hand, raunch can be the basis for a scene filled with humiliation or it might be one of significant intimacy, of getting in touch with primal and/or infantile forces and feelings, or simply one of iconoclasm, letting yourself loose from societal norms and expectations. It's easy to see that a scene of dominance and submission can be enhanced by the top's pissing or spitting on his bottom. The motives for giving and receiving such attention are the assertion of power over another or of submission. At other times such activity may fulfill a desire to get in touch with one's darker side, to experience the forbidden, the outlawed, or the outlandish.

Not all such activity, though, needs to be thought out. Sometimes we do things just because we feel like doing them. The food fight scenario, for instance, isn't the most logical of all actions but can release a significant amount of tension and create a strong sense of freedom and joy. Face it, there are times when we just need to let loose.

Let loose? Did I say let loose?

One of the most abhorred SM activities is scat. Interestingly though, it is one of the topics that my readers, over the years, have requested. It seems that a lot of people want to know about it, even as they turn up their noses at the thought of doing such a thing. Before any of you tell me you want to shit on me in the near future, let me say that it's not one of my fetishes. I don't do scat, though enema scenes do turn me on. Yes, I have done scat so I can speak from experience, but it's not my usual form of sexual and sadomasochistic expression.

In each of five scenes I was the giver and in four of them I did the shitting because it was requested by my partner. Two of the times (did I say once?) when I did it, it turned me on, two were somewhat neutral, and one made me feel disgusted, dirty, and sick that I had done such a thing.

It was the disgusting scene that turned out to be the most enlightening. I remember that after it was over I felt dirty. I couldn't wait to get home and take a shower. I spent a good deal of time afterwards talking with my friend Jim D. His friendship and dialogue helped me to re-center myself and come back from the feelings with which the action had left me. By shitting at my partner's request, I got in touch with the psychic, emotional, and spiritual sides of defecation. I realized why there are such taboos regarding human feces. Certainly those taboos stem from very serious concerns about matters of health.

Beyond that though, there is a great deal of unfortunate negativity about the very essential body functions of waste elimination. I am of the opinion that our bodies are beautiful creations of loving and wise god(s?). As such, each of our natural functions is marvelous and sacred.

You all, I'm sure, remember the part in science class about the food chain. It is the wonderful system that demonstrates how all of us, every species and kind, are interdependent: the minerals, vegetables, and animals with whom we share this fragile planet. What the food chain shows, of course, is a very anthropocentric outlook. You know, man is the center of the universe, or in this case, at the top of the chain. That schematic isn't necessarily so. Shit is a primary element that we give to the food chain. Our fecal matter is a gift of nourishment returned to the earth. Just as Mother Nature feeds us with grain, fruit, and meat, so too we feed the planet with our defecation. Rather than being ugly, scat is a beautiful and holy fact of life. What made this unpleasant encounter so distressful was that I saw it as a break in the food chain, a lack of honor to the planet. Instead of returning to the earth what she deserved, I was interrupting normal biological processes (that is, fertilizing the earth) for dangerous, selfishly erotic purposes. Basically, though, my reaction wasn't so much reasonable as emotional and hence is more difficult to explain. That, of course, only happened to me once and I think, in retrospect, that the adverse feelings were aroused more by our attitudes than our actions.

The other four scat scenes didn't hold such disgust. I remember that, like the food chain, they had a strong component of sharing. There was a recognition as well, unspoken but nevertheless present, that we were honoring our connection to the earth, rather than breaking it. Sharing is an integral part of much of human activity. There isn't much that we do that doesn't involve sharing. Sharing is a significant part of raunch.

In fact, the best raunch scenes hold such attraction because the sharing of bodily products (sweat, spit, urine, and shit) includes an incredible intimacy. We identify those elements with both self and other and find ways, i.e., rubbing, tasting, drinking, smelling, to identify the gift with the giver.

There is pleasure in the giving. Pissing, for instance, can be almost as much fun as coming. Certainly there is no denying that relieving one's bladder feels good. My partners have used receiving as a strong erotic force. I know, for instance, that tasting sweat or feeling the hot rush of urine on one's chest is arousing and satisfying. Some even say that the smell of sweat has the same effect as poppers.

It's easy to write off raunch as simply disgusting, but the truth is that there are significant pros and cons to such activity. Getting in touch with one's real feelings and honoring the beauty of our bodies are important actions. It doesn't, of course, mean that you need raunch, but let me be the first to say "Don't knock it if you haven't tried it."

Sado-Mastery and
Maso-Submission

April 08, 2007

Iapologize for using a cute title, but I like it. On the other hand I have no intention of adding two more words to our vocabulary so please don't get the idea that you ought to begin calling yourself or, worse yet, insist that others call you "Sir Sado-Master." (The author wrote while laughing.)

My friend and fellow club brother, whom I'll call Mr. Benson because he asked me to, has been involving me in a delightful conversation about slave searching. It seems that he is corresponding with an applicant who wrote about mastery and pain. The discussion entailed whether or not Dominance and Sadism were always, often, or seldom paired.

Reflecting on my own experience, I admit to being a sadist, simply because inflicting pain on my partner arouses me. For me, there is a direct, yet very inexplicable, connection between pain and sexual arousal. That, of course, would lead most everyone to the conclusion that Patrick, having been on the receiving end of my sadism, is a masochist. After more than eleven years as my partner, he will say, as he always has, that he is not. Likewise, I would agree.

Analysis of an action implies that we first must dissect the activity into its component parts. Doing so means that the action we are investigating is destroyed, just as when we dissect a frog, we look only at frog parts since the living, acting frog is now dead. Please keep that in mind as I discuss four interrelated fetishes.

The first two are Sadism and Masochism, wherein sexual arousal is based on pain. In our subculture the fetish itself is highly constrained by our dedication to safety and to a "good trip." Therefore our sadomasochism is altered by such things as preparation, warm-ups, sensitivity to the reaction of the bottom, safe-words, and aftercare. This, I maintain, is a good thing.

Actual sadism, on the other hand, would hardly include any of this. Instead the sadist would just as well inflict immediate, dangerous, and even deadly pain upon the person who would in fact become a victim rather than a partner. I write this because I can confess to what my fantasy life desires, with the full knowledge that I will not do such things. Not every fantasy ought to be explored to its more hideous depths. Likewise, there are masochists who fantasize about such darkness but who have the rational self-restraint not to go there.

The second two are Domination and Submission, reflected in control on the one hand and obedience on the other. Though we don't often consider the fact, these two can easily be separated from Sadomasochism. There are some or many (where are the scientific polls when you need them?) who enter a D/s relationship without any infliction of pain. Sissy maids come to mind here, though I am sure there are others whose relationship reflects D/s without SM.

Where, then, do D/s and SM meet? Certainly there are those partners where all four fetishes are present: the top is sadistic and controlling, the bottom masochistic and submissive. In fact, most Master/slave couples (and Top/bottom couples as well) appear to be in such a relationship. Let me remind you that appearances can be deceiving. I think that just such a deception might be seen in my relationship with Patrick since, as I noted, he frequently appears to be on the receiving end of my sadism.

For his part, if you ask him, Patrick will say that he is not a masochist, though he has learned to tolerate pain quite well, if it is administered in a safe and sane way. He will tell you that he does not enjoy the pain itself but he greatly enjoys the enjoyment that he knows I receive when he accepts my sadistic activity. His pleasure, then, is not found in the pain but in the enjoyment of serving me. Giving me pleasure is his pleasure.

For my part, careful analysis of my sexual activity (who wants to be a fly on my bedroom wall?) might show that I am not as sadistic as I think, though I will most certainly not rule out the fact that I am a sadist, as noted in the above description of my fantasy life. I have come to understand that my primary, but by no means sole, fetish is control. Let's look at the indications that such is a fact.

When asked by prospective partners what I want most, I tell them that I want to be in control. I tell slave applicants that what I want is obedience. In fact I have them learn a dialogue that goes like this:

Q. "What are you?"
A. "A slave, Sir."
Q. "Who am I?"
A. "A (or My) Master, Sir."
Q. "Why are you here?"
A. "For your sadistic pleasure, Sir."
Q. "What do I want?"
A. "Obedience, Sir."
Q. "What will you give me?"
A. "Pleasure, Sir."
Q. "How?"

A. "By obeying you, Sir."
Q. "Why?"
A. "Because my obedience gives you pleasure, Sir."

I then end the dialogue by saying "If you obey me, then I will get everything else that I want."

Sadistic activity, then, which indeed gives me pleasure in and of itself, perhaps gives me even more pleasure as an expression of my control over my partner. It is the control, I think, that is even more arousing than the sadism. This concept is confirmed by observation of other of my actions during sex. For instance, I often forbid Patrick or Matthew from sucking my cock, simply because I enjoy the idea that I can forbid them. I stick my fingers in their assholes because I see it as a violation of their bodies, something I do, as I tell them, "Because I can and you can't stop me."

I have, on numerous occasions, reminded Patrick that he has no right to stop me, as he has given me all his rights. "Slaves don't have rights," I'll say. "Your rights are mine. I am in control." Another similar dialogue is:

Q. "Who's in control, Patrick?"
A. "You are, Sir?"
Q. "Why, Patrick?"
A. "Because you are my master, Sir."
Q. "Why Patrick?"
A. Because I am your slave, Sir."
Q. "Why, Patrick?"
A. "Because slaves need to be controlled, Sir."

As illustrated below, being controlled is high on Patrick's agenda.

This was driven home to both of us some two or three years ago, at the resolution of a period during which we were having some difficulties during sex. We spent quality time, for well over more than six months, discussing why there was a problem. It was Patrick who eventually diagnosed it properly. It seems, and he was right, that over time I had begun controlling him less and he resented this fact. The solution was that he admitted to me that he wanted more control and I found ways to exercise it. This, I think, points to the clear fact that our relationship is based more (though certainly not entirely) on the D/s continuum rather than the SM one.

Indeed, I have had many partners for whom SM is important and even some for whom D/s is not desired. Though I love playing with a heavy masochist, it is the obedient bottom who satisfies me the most. Like my sadism, though, this is just as inexplicable. I hope that writing about it gives us all food for thought and leads to a better understanding of why we play (to use the common euphemism) as we do.

78

My Favorite Fetish

April 16, 2007

The previous chapter leads quite naturally into a discussion of control, which is a strong motivator for me and my favorite fetish. Exercising control arouses me, though I'll hasten to add not in all circumstances. On the other hand, even when being in control isn't arousing I find it very satisfying. Why that is the case I'll leave for others to decide. For me it simply is part and parcel, perhaps even the essence, of who I am. It is certainly a strong personality trait, a significant motivator, a source of pleasure, and a strong component of my self-image.

My handy Webster defines the verb "control" as "to exercise restraining or directing influence over: regulate; to have power over: rule." We can see then that it is very much part of the power dynamic in which we kinky people participate. As a word, "control" can be applied to both tops and bottoms of all kinds across the continuum of play. Negotiation is meant to define the scope of influence and the degree of power. The scene becomes the expression of that agreed-upon control, as it is in long-term relationships as well.

Let's look, then, at some of the aspects of control as it contributes to a healthy expression of one's identity.

As I stated above, control is always part of a relationship. Since all relationships have some kind of structure, even if that structure is short term, control is the mechanism that creates the structure, though often the restraint or direction comes not from the individuals but from other controlling factors. Gravity, for instance, controls what we do. Other controlling factors are the law, dungeon masters and scene rules, physical limitations and abilities, and constraints such as time, money, and venue.

Between individuals factors such as trust, fear, prior experience, fantasy, and confidence influence the degree of control that will be present. So we give less control to someone who is relatively unknown to us, and more to a trusted partner with whom we have had positive experiences. Negative experiences will cause us to cede less control, while desire for a life of abject slavery may cause us to give over more control, at least in the short term.

For us who understand the value of safe, sane, and consensual, agreement is a necessary part of creating the control dynamic. That means the extent of control is negotiated. It is neither assumed nor presumed. It is articulated and understood. The control that is exercised is limited by the definition of what can and cannot be influenced by the one in control.

The degree and areas of control seem to flow from one's personality, so that we are naturally dominant or submissive, though it is obvious that where and how those personality traits are manifest is highly dependent upon external forces. Therefore the expression of one's dominance may be limited at work but active at home, or vice versa. Psychologists have terms to describe other traits, such as extrovert and introvert, or passive and aggressive, and indeed multiple personality traits are going to determine the extent and areas of control. Jung spoke of these traits in terms of archetypes, so that a person's unconscious might involve the King (a dominant archetype) or the slave (obviously a submissive one).

Another way to look at control is to understand that control has benefits. At last week's Master And slaves Together meeting, my friend Bobby, a slave to my friend David, spoke in glowing terms of how happy he is to have been collared. He finds his slavery liberating. It gives him a sense of belonging and of security. Likewise my slave Patrick acknowledges his own need to be controlled and has actively sought to be controlled. He, too, is happy in having created that kind of relationship.

On the other hand, there are many, I am sure, who chafe because they are controlled unwillingly. I was in a discussion recently with a man who said he once had a partner who read his email and searched the text messages on his cell phone in an effort to control him -- without his negotiated consent. As a submissive he had just accepted such controlling actions without discussion or agreement, though obviously not without resentment and a feeling of being repressed.

Control can be manipulative, secretive, and repressive, as illustrated above, or it can be acknowledged and liberating, as noted by Bobby and Patrick. As are many qualities, control itself is neutral. It is the application of control that determines its appropriateness and its goodness. Generally speaking it is the extremes of control, either too much restriction or none at all, that are dangerous. That the healthy life is a balanced one applies to control as much as anything else. When we carefully investigate a healthy D/s relationship we see supportive, empowering and agreed-upon control. When we look at any abusive relationship we find control that is repressive and nonconsensual.

That then leads me to my next axiom: "Everyone has an agenda." Control is always part of our relationships because it is only by regulating and directing our lives, and hence those in it, that we can obtain that for which we seek. I want, for example, to teach my students, so I take control of my classroom. For their part they want to learn so they cede that control to me.

It becomes necessary, then, to understand that control is going to be according to one's purpose and that those purposes may not, in fact, be stated. Over the years I have learned to state my agenda as clearly as possible upon entering into a discussion about my fantasies. Hence, I teach slave applicants that I want obedience, which is another way of saying that an intimate relationship with me involves a great deal of control. Unfortunately most people confuse what I say with what they want to hear, thinking that I am only speaking about a scene, not a lifestyle.

When, therefore, I tell them they must do something outside of the scene (wash the dishes, take out the garbage, go to bed), they realize that the degree of control I seek is not the same as theirs and the discussion ends. Here we can see where defining the scope of influence becomes important, even though many people often forget to discuss it.

There are a great many forms in which control may be expressed and each of us must find the structures and definitions that best suit us. Only by understanding the nature and purpose of control can we realize which forms are most appropriate, indeed most authentic, to a healthy expression of our selves.

Relationships

How To Make Good Sex Better

February 26, 2002

Living in a sex-negative culture has its price. It generally means that we are bereft of positive images about sex, have little really helpful instruction about technique, and are left to our own devices when it comes to self-improvement. My own education about sex came from a library book that my high school friend Jack had borrowed and then lent to me. It gave me a heads-up biologically speaking, but there is a lot more to sex than biology and not very many ways to learn it. What passed for sex education when I was in high school was nothing more than a sexually-repressed morality lesson, mostly condemning masturbation and pre-marital intercourse.

But hey, when you think that sex is only for procreation you don't need to make it satisfying or enjoyable. Too often we end up groping our way along (excuse the pun) trying to figure out what works best and searching for ideas that add spice to what otherwise can become a very routine and unsatisfying event.

Good sex begins with and in our minds. Our brain is our largest sex organ and the best piece of equipment we have to insure that our sex is as good as it can be. That said, we can use our minds by reflecting, discussing, planning, and learning what works.

For starters, then, reflect on your own attitudes about sex. What are your hang-ups? What sex-negativity do you bring to the dungeon or bedroom? Are sex organs dirty? Is kissing for sissies? Are certain body parts "off limits"? Is sex a duty or a drag? Not really something you want to do? How do you feel afterwards? Is there any hint of embarrassment, guilt, shame, or frustration?

If you can answer "Yes" to the idea that you have some negative thoughts about sex, then the first step is to recognize them and find ways to deal with them. Here I'm going to have to leave you to your own devices, as I certainly can't tell you what to do about your thoughts. Counseling, sharing, discussions, reading, and observing others all are ideas you might want to try. Ask for and seek help. It's as simple as that.

Secondly I think it's important to understand the individuality of sexuality. What's right for you is specifically geared to you.

Remember too that porno movies don't give any indication whatsoever as to what is normal or even actual. Those films are filled with actors, and hours' worth of filming is thrown away just to give the viewer an edited film that includes only the best parts. Porn films, like novels, are not full of realistic sex. Don't use them as role models. Not every sexual encounter is going to be filled with bells and whistles. Some nights we are just too tired or too hassled. Don't load every sexual moment with unrealistic expectations.

Mom's right when she says "It takes two to tango." Your sex life can be improved by talking about it with your partner. Choose a non-threatening place to do it and make sure that you ask open-ended questions, and listen carefully to any responses. Solicit ideas from each other and give your partner a chance to respond. Let him or her share from the heart and do your best to do the same. This discussion is no time to be shy. It may be difficult to bring up your most secret fantasy but if you don't ask, you won't receive. Remember that how you feel reflects your feelings, not something that your partner is projecting onto you. Take responsibility for your own emotions and hang-ups. No one "makes" you feel a certain way. Those are your feelings, created from within yourself.

There are times, of course, when it might be appropriate to bring a neutral third party into the discussion, especially when you both feel the need for a referee or mentor. You may, for instance, want to find a third person to teach both of you a new technique. This can happen at a workshop, informally in a play space, or by asking an expert for some private tutoring. Again, if you don't ask, you'll never receive.

Talking all this to death hardly provides a complete solution. Once you can agree on change, you need to plan for it. Maybe you'll need to go on a shopping spree together to get ideas and a new toy. Perhaps you'll want to build a new piece of equipment for the bedroom or spend some time reading a book together. Remember that better sex takes planning. The best scenes are ones where all of the components work: the space sets the right mood with lighting, heat, equipment, and music; you have the time set aside to do it right, without interruption or the need to rush; and you have already negotiated limits so that you can trust one another.

Partners who live together may have to actually set a time and place. Go on a date, put it on your calendar, make it a priority as you would any special event. If you just expect it to happen without any effort, you're going to be grossly disappointed.

The need to trust cannot be overstated. If there are hidden issues, secrets, and unspoken difficulties between you and your partner, they are going to adversely affect your sex. Even when you think the secret is too hidden to have an effect, it will. Dishonesty in any form will eventually cripple your sex life, even if it is never spoken or in any way acknowledged.

The bedroom is no place to discuss your fears and doubts,

but you do need to deal with them as best you can, when you can. Better sex happens when the partners are sure that the "air is clear" between them.

Once you get to the sex act, whatever that may mean, remember that speed counts. By and large, the less speed, the better. Start slowly and allow your foreplay to build over time. Take breaks to cuddle and rest. The idea is to work your way towards a crescendo, relax, and then start up again. Having an orgasm is not necessarily the objective here. Mutual pleasure is.

I like to include a number of different techniques in my sex play so I'm liable to do some spanking, flogging, bondage, tit play, sucking, fucking, and lots of kissing and touching, not necessarily in that order. Be willing to experiment. When doing so, start slowly, do just a little bit of the activity, and then take a moment to see if you both want to try more of it. Agreeing to try something is not a promise you'll like it or even that you will do it more than once. On the other hand, if you don't try it you'll never know if you like it as you'll have nothing more than your prejudice to guide you.

Some things, of course, take getting used to. Give new ideas a chance. Likewise, don't force your ideas on an unwilling partner as that is only going to get you into trouble.

Lastly, take some time, outside the bedroom and dungeon, after the fact, to do a mutual de-briefing. Learn from each other what went well and what you both liked as well as what went wrong, might need improvement, or that one or both of you didn't like. You and your partner, after all, are going to be your own best teachers.

Just Say No

September 13, 2006

Mark wrote what I thought was an interesting email. I hope you think it's interesting as well: "I've been confused about whether as a slave I should probably pretty much submit to the next guy who comes along. (And I'm often tempted to, especially since I'm 47 and I've wanted something like this for some 35 years...ugh!) Just a couple days ago, I felt bad after just one email with a gentleman, when I thanked him for his response to my ad, but HINTED that I thought we might be incompatible and he responded in part thusly: 'maybe you will come to understand that becoming a slave means giving up your own preferences for how you live and serve as a slave and instead adopt the preferences of your master.'"

As with many of our BDSM relationships (and many other ones as well) this email indicates some of the nearly devastating myths that plague us Leatherfolk. I try my best to demythologize what it is that we do but it often seems like an impossible task. Part of that process for me, for instance, is that I edit emails that I am going to use in my column.

In the above quotation I changed all the incorrect uses of "i" from lower case to upper case and all the uses of "Him" and "He" to lower case. For two strangers to begin a conversation using incorrect capitalization sends the wrong message. Neither Mark nor his master-applicant should be subservient in any way to the other, nor, need I add, superior.

I write this because I believe that all negotiations, and I mean all, must be conducted between adults who recognize each other's equality. I will not agree to anything less than the clear acknowledgment of the equality of all players. To be sure we are different; each of us is unique, but that in no way implies inequality. If two people don't negotiate as peers then there can be no honest negotiation, since the one will always be either deferring to the other and the other will have the unfair advantage of assumed "superiority."

This is an important point. Authority, demonstrated by the assertion of control, must never be assumed. It is negotiated. Authority is only granted to the top/dominant as a gift, that which is freely given, by the bottom/submissive. I am not limiting this discussion to D/s relationships. All our relationships must reflect this dynamic of choice and gift, else they begin (if only in the smallest part) to become coercive.

So Mark's master-applicant was offended that Mark hinted they might not be compatible. Mark had every right to say so. Indeed he (and all of us) have an obligation to say so. In my book, it's better to end the negotiations sooner rather than later, so that both are saved a real waste of time.

All those thoughts simply flow out of the misuse of capitalization. What more was going on in the dialogue? What other myths plagued the correspondence? I only have part of the email so there is not much more to go on, except for the master-applicant's statement that "maybe you will come to understand that becoming a slave means giving up your own preferences for how you live and serve as a slave and instead adopt the preferences of your master."

I have no argument with the idea that "becoming a slave means ... adopt[ing] the preferences of your master." To think that two people can enter into any kind of relationship without some kind of compromise, some melding of preferences and habits, is a wholly unrealistic expectation. Of course partners are going to change their lives in such a way as to accommodate one another. Depending upon the extent of the dominance and submissiveness in the relationship, the accommodation will be more from one and less from the other.

For the most part, of course, human relationships are built upon mutual accommodation. There is give and take on both sides. At other times, one party is more dominant than the other. My students, for instance, sign up for and agree to attend my classes, hence I expect them to change their behavior to match the criteria listed in my syllabus. See? I told you that we could speak about these things in "any kind of relationship." Leather is, after all, a human relationship.

Those who fail to remember that both kinky folk in a relationship are human are destined to a harsh wake up call when they discover that the top or bottom of their dreams is less than perfect. What that master-wannabe failed to realize is that there are always two very separate criteria at work in the creation of a relationship. Here I use the word relationship with a lower case "r" as it applies to all relationships, even ones that last as little as a fifteen-minute scene in a public dungeon.

The first is the definition of the relationship itself without regard to the "other" of the relationship. It is, in that regard, like the decision to be an accountant or a veterinarian or a delivery man. We evaluate ourselves with the intention of knowing our own being-ness. The question that first must be answered has nothing at all to do with the potential partner with whom one is negotiating, but rather has everything to do with you. Until you know what you want you will not be able to fully negotiate what you want with the other person. I don't want you to take this further than it is meant. You can, after all, know just a little of what you want and negotiate that "little."

It should be obvious that the second aspect is the appropriateness of the person who will share in what it is that you want. Using the examples listed above, not every employer is a potential employer for that accountant, veterinarian, or delivery man. Why then do we think that every flogger (as in the person doing the flogging) is the right flogger? Why should every master-applicant think that all slave-applicants should be his or hers? They shouldn't. It is as simple as that. Why should any player assume a superiority over any other? They shouldn't. There is much to be said here about the necessity of equality in our negotiations as well as in every other aspect of living. Inequality has no place in the lives of kinky players, not even in a D/s relationship.

Ah, here is the explosion of another myth. Masters and slaves are equal, even if their roles appear otherwise. Think of it this way: the bolt needs the nut, the nail the hammer, the tree tops their roots, the masculine the feminine, the inserter the insertee, the convex, the concave. Such is the dance of this universe.

The fact which that master-applicant missed is that becoming a master means being willing to change one's life just as surely as it demands that the slave-applicant change. The creation of relationship is the mutual acceptance of change. Sure, the slave will become subservient, controlled, and directed. Just as importantly the master will become responsible, caring, and directing. Unless both understand the import of what they do, their relationship won't work. Until we know what we want and find the right person with whom to create that reality, it is better to say "No thanks" than to walk blindly into the wrong relationship.

Anger

May 31, 2004

One of the less discussed situations among us is the presence of anger, "a feeling of extreme displeasure, hostility, indignation, or exasperation toward someone or something; rage; wrath; [or] ire," according to my faithful American Heritage Dictionary. To try to write about it in an essay this short will leave much unsaid, so please bear with me and use this column as a mere starting point to learn, grow, and improve. Please don't get angry with me that it's not longer, more complete, or fully satisfying.

Having started thusly, many players will note that we don't see much anger in our dungeons. That is true and as it should be. As I've written many times before, a play space is never an appropriate place for exhibiting anger, nor many other negative forces that too often dwell in the human heart. Play spaces are for pleasure, though play in itself can be more than just pleasurable. Play can be a learning, cathartic, or bonding experience. It can also be therapeutic, though I will again hasten to add that our dungeons and bedrooms ought not to be used as areas for therapy.

The fact that we don't often see anger (or rather the exhibition of it) in our dungeons belies the fact that it is still present. Feelings need not be revealed, and very often, in our dreadfully repressed society, they aren't.

That, of itself, is not necessarily bad. After all, sublimation, delay, and discretion are appropriate ways to deal with all sorts of issues. There is a time for every purpose under heaven so there's certainly an appropriate time and place to express anger, just as there are inappropriate moments and venues. Knowing the difference is important.

The easy part of this topic deals with the quick, reactive expression of anger in a scene, as when a bottom has just gotten one hit or hurt too many and explodes in a momentary tirade. Such a release may lead to a great deal of catharsis ("A purifying or figurative cleansing or release of the emotions or of tension, esp. through art"). This is a healthy effect of what we do, though it is hardly predictable.

In most cases we can easily deal with such a release. The

top needs simply to take a moment, step back and breathe, then gently approach the bottom in a comforting and reassuring way, encouraging him or her to relax, lighten up, and breathe deeply as well. That done, it is imperative that the top discern, through questioning or experience, what might have provoked the unwanted expression and rectify it. Such a burst may mean the scene ends but often it simply means that the scene has to be modified in some way.

Quick outbursts, to be sure, are not plentiful, though they probably happen more often in private play than public. I should also note that they can in fact be welcome and included in the scene. If that is the case then it is imperative that such be clearly understood by both participants and, if there is a Dungeon Master, by him or her as well.

I enjoy pushing my partner to the point of explosion. After all, I'm a mean and sadistic son of a bitch. Like the rest of us, I get most of my pleasure from the reaction, not necessarily the actions that provoke it. In any case it is important that the angry reaction be addressed in a positive and supportive way. If indeed you are seeking a reaction, you have to be ready for it and attend to it with understanding, patience and care. You also should know for certain that your provocations are welcome and not a violation of what you have negotiated. Additionally, to merely provoke the anger and ignore it will damage the both the scene and the relationship. That said, good after care between the players is the perfect time to insure that all, in spite of appearances, is well.

The more difficult aspect of "anger management" deals with long-term, chronic, and often-denied anger. This may not be serious and may be easily dealt with or it may require counseling or therapy. Universities often give workshops in anger management and if an individual's problem warrants it, I recommend availing oneself of such a course of action.

I know of a woman who was constantly expressing inappropriate anger, even towards those who were her friends. Her un-attended rage was leveled chaotically and often, leading to her dismissal at work. Her union did its best to rescue her employment and she was offered an employer-paid anger management seminar. Unfortunately she was too angry to see its value and was thus forced to express herself at another workplace. Some people are so blinded by their anger that resolving it is nearly impossible.

As I continue this essay I need to remind my readers that I am not a professional counselor and that I can only scratch the surface of this issue. I can, though, recommend that if you think that anger is a problem for you, your friend, your family, or your organization, there are ways to deal with it constructively.

The first, of course, is to acknowledge that it exists. Like my former friend above, denial will certainly worsen the situation. Unfortunately we too often see denial as some kind of easy, short-term solution. There comes a time when denial is no longer possible and that which is ignored takes center stage. They don't say "A stitch in time saves nine" for nothing. Better deal with a small wound than a major festering.

Though we seldom realize it, there is nothing wrong, in itself, with anger. It is a natural human emotion. It is part and parcel of who we are. The "wrong" flows not from the anger but from how we express it. If we but find ways to divert the anger from harm to growth, it can be a powerful remedy and a healthy release.

Therefore I encourage people that the anger be first acknowledged. Doing so can then lead to its expression in a safe and protected way. More than once we have sought a good flogging or spanking to help us safely and surely release the feelings of rage, wrath, or ire. I have been known to go into my room, close the door, and beat a pillow because I felt angry. Having felt the feelings I am better able then to begin to understand them.

This is really the critical part of the process. In many cases our anger, expressed in one direction, is really anger diverted from another object. My former friend, for instance, was seldom really angry at any of us, as we were the union trying to help her. On the other hand, she often vented her anger at one of us in language that vilified another of us, never coming to the conclusion that the true source of her anger was elsewhere.

This is why, after acknowledgment, it is critically important that we analyze in order to gain clarity about the what and why of our feelings. Revealing the roots of the anger can be a difficult process, yet one that will yield enormous benefits.

At a recent seminar I was asked about techniques for coming to this knowledge. They are many and include personal reflection and meditation, journaling, professional counseling, and discussion with a trusted and responsible friend, mentor, or guide. Self-expression through art and crafts, exploration through education, reading, and research are other avenues of growth.

It is important that we see all of this as a process of unlayering, much like you can strip away the layers of an onion, the removal of one revealing the next, as we move carefully toward the innermost core of our (the onion's?) center. That is the purpose, in my humble opinion, of life: for each to find his or her center and rest there in tranquil delight. Getting over our anger is part and parcel of the process.

Expectations

September 05, 2006

There are lots of reasons that relationships "work," but it seems to me that one of the more important qualities of successful partners is that they have mutual expectations that are both realistic and understood. Expectations enter into both the creating and the maintaining of a successful relationship. Lover-hunting can be hindered by the kind of expectations you have in your search. If you set, for instance, all sorts of limits on who the lucky person's going to be, falling in love, or whatever you want to call it, may just never happen.

A man from New York heard that I was helping masters and slave applicants to meet each other, so he wrote to ask what kind of slaves I have "for sale." That's a laugh in itself as I should be so lucky as to have some to sell, so I wrote back asking him what kind of slave he was seeking. His answer brought another laugh: "I would like a slave less than 35 years old, preferably with red hair. This can be discussed when you find someone. I am not looking for a perfect body, I can change whomever I get."

First off, if I knew an under-35-year-old red-headed slave, I wouldn't sell him. My desires are to have men just like that serve me, though I have to admit to dreaming about one with red hair, one with blond, one with black, etc. You get the idea. Like any other lust-filled fool, I want a stable of Colt men under the age of thirty.

To start, it's important to separate one's wants from one's expectations. Failing to do so may quite well leave you in the position of looking right in the eyes of your perfect mate and seeing someone whom you completely reject. I know a searching Master, for instance, who wants a younger slave but fully admits that his favorite fuck-buddy is over the age of sixty and that his one successful long-term relationship was with a person his own age, which is hardly under thirty. In this case he would be well-advised to adjust his expectations. Failing to do so will most likely mean that he'll never find a partner that really suits him.

But there's more to expectations than youth and big cocks. A recent slave applicant, for instance, is a switch. During our conversation about the possibly of his becoming my slave, he mentioned a hesitancy based on his expectation that as my slave he would no longer be allowed to top another slave. In this case his expectation was based on his interpretation of the situation. It was certainly not a mutual expectation.

Now this is a guy who has read my writings extensively. I therefore asked him why he thought that way and reminded him that nowhere had I ever said or written that one slave couldn't top another. From my experience I know that it happens all the time. Masters love to watch slaves suck or fuck one another. Some even go so far as to have one slave beat the other. You see what I mean. Misunderstood expectations stand in the way of developing relationships.

Unfortunately we seem to spend a great amount of time misunderstanding each other. Some of that, I'm convinced, is because we don't even try to understand each other. We'd just rather keep on blathering along, seldom if ever giving the other a chance to explain or prove, hardly ever listening to them.

A slave applicant whom I am mentoring sent an email to someone who had posted an ad. Without so much as a phone call or a series of questions to ascertain the slave's ability, the want-to-be Master wrote back: "There is no way you could keep up with the physical demands I put a slave through, sorry slave boy." That was his expectation concerning the applicant. But upon what, pray tell, did he based his conclusion? I know for a fact, since I have tried this slave, that he is a pain pig, incredibly zealous to please, and willing to do Anything, and I mean Anything with a capital "A," to please. Notice here that I tried out the slave. One cannot base a relationship, be it short term or long, on conjecture. Experience is not only the best teacher, it's most likely the only teacher.

That is a great lead into my favorite story. When I was a young adolescent we lived on a very busy highway which I was long forbidden to cross. One summer my mother finally gave me permission to cross by myself, and I did. I crossed the street, climbed up the embankment, ran across the fields, and found several gullies, each of which contained a small stream. Before long I learned that some of the stones in the streams hid salamanders. That summer "salamandering" became my obsession and a lifelong lesson. The more rocks I turned over, the more salamanders I found.

Now there wasn't a salamander under every rock. Many rocks hid none at all, but the lesson was still the same: The more rocks I turned over, the more salamanders I found. One couldn't, of course, tell what was under the rock by looking at the top of it. One's expectation concerning the number of salamanders under the rock was totally irrelevant to what one caught. But if you didn't turn the rock over because you didn't expect it to be hiding a salamander, that meant that there could be one lucky salamander under that very rock who wouldn't be found that day.

That master wannabe who wouldn't try out the slave's endurance let his expectations obliterate his chance to get one of the strongest and most devoted slaves he'll ever meet.

Expectations don't only muck up prospective relationships. They can do a mean job on present ones, even long term present ones. The gentleman who's looking for the redhead makes a telling claim when he writes "I can change whomever I get." Believe me, the world is filled with unhappy marriages based on the idea that one partner can change the other.

My mother had that expectation for me.

A month or so before our marriage, my fiancée and her parents came to our home for the traditional meet-each-other dinner, during which my mother, god bless her, turned to my wife-to-be and said, "Ann, I'm so glad you're marrying my son because I know you'll make a man out of him." Talk about unrealistic expectations! I had them too. After all, the nuns had taught me well and I knew [read "foolishly" in there someplace] that getting married would alleviate my concupiscence. Well, it didn't. And if you don't know what that means, get out your dictionary.

Seriously though, what kind of expectations do you have for your relationships? What kind of expectations do you have when you cruise the bars, go to work, attend a play party, surf the web, or sit at the keyboard in a chat room? All that's to say, make your expectations realistic and make them understood. Doing so will bring you a world of successes wherever you find your wants and desires taking you.

Earned, Not Requested

February 14, 2005

I'll try to keep my comments on the helpful side, rather than sliding into a rant. Here is the comment that sparked my writing: "I have recently become a Sir (in my own right). Although I am in a well-known chat room, it surprises me that when I decided to become a Sir some of the fairly well known so called 'Masters' and 'Sirs' there were not quite ready to see my transformation. I had been a slave and a boy for a very long time but yet they were not 'prepared' to see me become 'one of them'."

First off, of course, is the question of what does Sir mean? According to my dictionary it is "A respectful form of address used instead of a man's name; A title of honor…; A gentleman of rank." A title, for our purposes, is "A formal appellation attached to a person or family by virtue of office, rank, hereditary privilege, noble birth, attainment, or as a mark of respect."

My first response is "How did you become a Sir?" Put another way, "What makes you a Sir?" You see, we are sometimes too quick to assume a title, when titles are, in fact, not really assumable. OK, you can do whatever you want on the keyboard of your computer, but there's nothing that says that saying it is so makes it so.

I think my reader is really trying to say that he has decided to favor his dominant characteristics. He is now a person who prefers to be in control in the situation, to exercise authority, to become a Sir to his or her partner. Any honest appraisal of the relationship patterns in our subculture will quickly prove that over the course of time, many, if not most, move along the dominant/submissive continuum and make similar changes in all sorts of ways and directions. Many, in fact, are switches and move along the continuum all the time.

Now if I am misreading the email and my correspondent has become a Sir because he has actually entered into a D/s relationship as the dominant partner, then it is merely a matter of letting his actions be seen. As he wrote "They were not 'prepared' to see me become 'one of them'." They are in fact "ready to see [his] transformation." All he has to do is demonstrate it by his actions.

There are two aspects to what we do. The first, in that it is a priori, is that one has the correct attitude. Attitude must then be made manifest, real, by action. If this person's kinky life is limited to a chat room, then there really is no more to say about the incident, except he only needs to get a new handle and appear in the chat room as a new person. He certainly won't be the first person in cyberspace to create a new identity!

I would venture, though, since he cared enough to ask, that there is more to all of this than fantasy. As is natural in the course of human life, he has come to a place where he wants to change his role as a Leather person. The first step in this is for him to accept his new self and to learn as much about what he wants to become as possible. Since he appears to be a person of experience in our lifestyle, I will assume he knows what it means to be a top.

If he looks like a top, walks like a top (I'm only kidding here), and acts like a top, people will begin to think of him as a top. There is one caveat here: it is difficult for a person to change an image held by a long-term acquaintance. Believe me, there are some people for whom I will always be "Joey." They've known me as that for many years and they're not about to begin calling me "Jack." Now the truth is that I don't like being called "Joey" but there's no dissuading my mother from using that name and I'm not even going to try.

The appropriateness of names and titles varies with the relationship as well. I expect, for instance, that a person who wants to be my slave will address me in a manner that reflects his intention and his hoped-for "rank" as my slave. I don't expect others to do the same. Like everyone else, I live in a number of different worlds. At the college where I teach, no one calls me Jack and no one needs to. I don't expect my close friends to call me "Mr. Rinella," even if one or two of them might do so on occasion. I enjoy calling Patrick my "bitch slave" when we are hot and heavy in a scene. I would never consider using that appellation if I were to greet him in his work place.

So my reader is well-known as a slave and a boy. Now his challenge is to let them see him as a master, daddy, or however he wants to manifest his Sir-ness. You see "There are many ways of thinking about power. One influential typology has identified five kinds of power in social groups: coercive power, reward power, legitimate power, referent power, and expert power" (from the book, *How Colleges Work, The Cybernetics of Academic Organization and Leadership*, by Robert Birnbaum).

Since he's not going to be able to coerce anyone into calling him Sir, he has to earn the title legitimately by having a submissive, thereby showing he knows how to live and act as a dominant, or by referral, which simply means that people see him as a dominant, refer to him as such and therefore lead others to do the

same.

I tell people to call me "Jack." If they find some reason to call me "Sir," "Master," or "Mr. Rinella," that is fine but I prefer to earn the title; hence I never ask for it, unless someone wants to become my slave. Then I request it as a sign that indeed they note my ability and have the desire to submit to me. At that point "Sir" becomes a sign of a growing relationship, one that I have with very few people.

We are, after all, better off as an egalitarian community. We need not assert ourselves over others to get what we want. In fact it is probably best that we don't. Instead we need to accept ourselves as we are, live according to that image, and let everyone else decide what title to use based on the way they see us live our lives. Friend, don't worry what they call you; be more concerned about how you live, and the titles naturally follow.

Jealousy

August 25, 1997

When I was a child we used to go to Uncle Mike's on Christmas Eve. Grandma was there and that made it convenient to see my Dad's side of the family. They opened their gifts then. After the visit we'd head to Midnight Mass and then home where my brother and I opened our gifts. On one particular night, my cousin Patty got a puppy. I still have vivid memories of that event, since it was the first time I remember feeling jealousy. I felt so jealous, in fact, that I felt I had to go to confession before I could go to communion.

Now, I'm not really sure if I was jealous or not. As I look back on what happened, it might have been envy. (My dictionary would define what I felt as envy.) In either case it hardly makes a difference some fifty years later. What made a difference was that I felt badly toward my cousin, whom I sure was oblivious to what her new puppy caused in me. The feelings I had were far from friendly. Oh, they passed with time and the fact that I eventually got my own dog, but it was hardly a moment appropriate to "Peace On Earth, Good Will Toward Men." No matter what ethical, religious, or moral values we hold, it seems that they all decry jealousy as an evil. Even in my post-Christian, neo-Pagan mindset, I can easily understand that.

Among us sexually active folks, jealousy can be a real problem. It's certain that it's a number one topic when readers ask me about the multiplicity of my relationships. "Doesn't Patrick get jealous of Matthew?" is a usual query.

Indeed, one of the foremost reasons for maintaining monogamy, or at least its appearance, is to avoid the pain that jealousy invokes. More than one relationship has been destroyed by a jealous lover.

When (my former Master) Lynn and I started this Leather family, it was begun on the premise that there was no room for jealousy. From the beginning we accepted and expected an open relationship, multiple partners, and a laissez-faire attitude toward other men and what we might do with them. Through the five years of being together we shared partners, introduced each other to others, and generally had no problem with jealousy.

Early on, my then lover Michael got occasionally bent out of shape about who was sleeping in my bed, but with time he learned both that no one would usurp his place in my heart and that it was fun to share one of my tricks once in a while anyway. He adjusted well to Patrick's slavery to me, learned to like Patrick, and to especially appreciate the perks that being a Master's lover brings. After all, when things got really tough, Michael could have Patrick do the laundry!

In considering why all this works as it does, there are several factors that come into play. Certainly the facts that open relationships were negotiated when we first met, that we were all older and had had our "monogamous years," and that we were committed to honesty plain and simple, all helped us to forebear being jealous.

Mostly, though, I've come to the conclusion that jealousy has more to do with one's self-esteem than anything else. We're jealous, it seems to me, because we are afraid of that which causes the feelings. It is our own insecurity that makes us feel jealous. Just because a lover has sex with another doesn't mean that I am no longer of any account in his heart, even if my fears tell me that might be the case. Yes, time spent with another is time I won't have with him or her, but to think that I can so completely do everything for a person that no others will be needed might be a rather far stretch of the imagination.

It boils down to a question of what fidelity means. To me it means being supportive, caring, interested; not wavering in our commitment to honesty, to mutual respect, to real consideration of the others' feelings. It takes some give and take, real compromise, and special consideration of the other's needs.

When, for instance, Patrick moved in with me, I made it a point to go beyond what Michael expected. Instead of getting his desired one night a week alone with me, I went to his home for two nights. His fear might have been that once Patrick was on the scene he'd see less of me. Instead he saw more of me. Another fear was that sex with Patrick would diminish my desire for him. In fact, the opposite happened.

How then do we best deal with jealousy? Remember that the lies that jealousy tells are just that. We are each good, acceptable, and satisfactory. No one is better (or less) than we. Yes, there are preferences, there are circumstances, there are (unfortunately) prejudices. In any case, in all cases, we have dignity, worth and honor as men and women who are worthy. Don't let the act that provokes jealousy make you think otherwise. Neither let your actions provoke jealousy. Be candid and forthright about your intentions, your needs, and your feelings. Find ways to show your faithfulness that will allay your partner's feelings of insecurity.

Fundamental to that, of course, is truthfulness. You're not going to defeat jealousy with deceit. If you can't discuss your feelings openly, without rancor and accusation, then you'll never get rid of the doubts that plague you. It is those doubts that breed jealousy and anger, even more than the actions themselves.

Another bit of advice is to do your best to insure that there are no surprises. After-the-fact admissions or (what's worse) discoveries aren't going to make for a happy relationship. That's why the first thing I do when I meet someone is to tell them about my partners. If a guy wants to be my slave I send him to my home page. Let him confront his feelings about Patrick and Matthew now, not later, while there are yet no feelings of "love" or "devotion."

Most of us, I think, make the mistake of falling in love. Love is a great feeling, and there ought to be more feelings like it, but the feeling too often blocks our other points of view. In love we lose a proper sense of our self, our values, our experiences, our rationality. All of a sudden the world is beautiful and any obstacle can be overcome. Unfortunately, the world doesn't operate that way and too soon the feelings leave us to face stark reality.

It is much easier to face reality before the trouble hits. The best way to avoid jealousy is well before it has a chance to start. In the beginning, when neither of you has an important emotional investment, learn what your mutual boundaries will be and how to communicate with each other.

Begin with honesty and sincerity and maintain that status at all costs. If that style doesn't work in the beginning there will be nothing lost as you go your merry, separate ways. If it does work, and it probably will, you'll be on the way to a relationship that will withstand almost any assault, even one of jealousy.

What Can Two Tops Do?

June 03, 2004

I am an incorrigible cruiser, as any of my friends will attest. In fact lots of strangers can do the same, as I firmly believe that if you don't ask, you don't get laid. I'm not even embarrassed that I put the moves on all sorts of people, as if my goal is to get a bad reputation. In my defense please let me say that I am very gracious at taking "No" for an answer, which is a good thing as most of my propositioning is greeted with a laugh.

In a good number of instances the reaction has been one of surprise as the target replies "Jack, you know I'm a top, what could we do together?" Therefore I have been formulating an answer over the years and now, thanks to Jason, I can give it to you. You're going to have to read this column with an eye to your own gender and orientation, even though I've gotten that "What" from both men and women, since I am an equal opportunity fucker, so to speak. That doesn't mean that two tops will fuck, as I am using the rather colorful word as somewhat of a catch-all.

Anyway, to all those out there who have asked me what we could do, here's the answer. But first the disclaimer: This column is not to be construed as listing everything that two tops can do nor that which they must do. You're going to have to read this as only a bit of inspiration, a kick in the butt to widen your perspective about this top and bottom thing. You may wish to only file it away until you are stranded on a desert island with only another top for company, since many tops are way too "something" (I want to use the word narrow-minded but won't lest I get in trouble with the folks who have turned me down) to have this answer at hand.

I met Jason at a fund-raiser at the Detroit Eagle and we hit it off quickly. Happily for me we had a nice conversation going long before he knew who I was. I don't even think he had ever heard of Jack Rinella before we shook hands at the bar. In any case we eventually began negotiating for a fling in my hotel room, even though it was soon obvious that we were both tops. Finding myself alone for another night I didn't let his topside turn me off, as if it would anyway. Whether we would make it or not took a bit

103

of figuring but we did. So what did we do?

For starters we got naked and cuddled and kissed and felt each other's skin and the organs underneath it. You know, I hope, that it's fun to be sensuous, passionate, and play kissy-face. I love to touch the private places of a man's testicles or a woman's labia, feeling the smoothness, the fleshiness, the heat of that which should not be touched. I enjoy lightly feeling up a dick head, an anus, or a tit, perhaps rubbing them between my thumb and forefinger.

I love to rub my hands on a chest, smooth or hairy, and on thighs or arms or a bald head. I love to feel long hair brush over me or the texture of short hair. "Hey give me a head of hair," they sang in the theater for good reason. I love the smell of a body, even of sweat, and the taste of another's skin. I guess that means you can put a good tongue licking on the list of what two tops can do. Have you figured out yet that all this is mutual? No wonder the number 69 is so popular, even if the action isn't mutual cocksucking.

That's not to say that two tops can't suck one another, as they most certainly can, and should. And, yes, that applies to you Het male tops as well, for whom I have only one sentence: Get over it. Reciprocal can be fun and don't knock it until you've tried it. As they say, if you didn't like it the first time, do it a second time just to be sure, then and only then you can write it off your list.

The advantage to this top on top thing is that we are both free to experiment and explore without worrying about what our bottom, submissive, boy, or slave will think. It's none of their business, quite frankly, thank you very much. So go ahead and give each other some head. Well, maybe not some; how about a lot of it?

Lick the shaft, taste the slit. Put your lips around the head and suck. Stroke the staff, smell the pre-cum. Feel free even to taste it. Suck up the balls lovingly and see how well they fill your mouth as you tickle his anus. The same goes if your fellow top isn't a fellow. Give her a good licking, sucking, and probing. This is after all, the twenty-first century.

If you're really getting into it, lube up the anal entry and play with it or wash it with spit and give it a good washing with your tongue. If you're lucky you may actually turn them on enough to make them willing to receive your dick or your finger where the sun doesn't shine.

Get the picture? By the end of the night (on our second date, not the first) I'm rubbing my hot and sweaty butt hairs all over his hard and wet penis. In a while I slip a condom on it, lube it up with KY, and sit right down on it. No kidding folks, a cock up the ass can feel good, even to a top like me. OK, especially to a top like me, though I don't want you all trying to hit on me THAT way all the time.

The truth is that sitting on a cock is mutual pleasure without the submission. I'm on top, I'm in control, and we're both having a good time. The speed, depth, and duration are all up to me, Yes, he's fucking me, but who's in charge? No one, we're just having a good time. Remember fun is why we do it?

So that's what two tops can do, and did, even if I left out the great dinner together, the amazing conversation, and the night's sleep cuddled in bed together. You see, the pick up trick turned into a second date, 'cause there's lots that two tops can do together, so quit asking dumb questions and come to my room.

Family as Driving Force

October 16, 2004

It's rather easy to characterize the subculture of Leather by its four-lettered abbreviation, BDSM. After all, this is an upfront, out loud, and unique hallmark of what we do. There are, other less-known aspects as well that often lie hidden under the boisterous side of our activities. Paramount among these is the quest for "Leather Family."

Family life has long been the strong support of human existence even if it wasn't "family" as caricaturized by the not-so-right wing. Through modern history, to be sure, family has always been more than the nuclear organization of husband, wife, and children. Family, in fact, is much more akin to clan.

The situation comedies of my youth spread the ridiculous idea that mom, dad, and kids were all it took, in spite of the fact that the Brady Bunch had Alice. Throughout history Father has seldom been the only one who knew best -- that task was left to the elders, who in some societies were female as well as male. Dad didn't bring home the bacon or the stew meat all by himself, either. He hunted with the tribe and mom worked outside the home: in the garden, at the river, and with the women of the village in hundreds of communal tasks.

So when we discuss family, let's not limit it to parents and 2.5 children. Hell --- my great-great-grandparents (married in 1820), as far as I can tell, had eight children. My father is one of eight; my maternal grandfather one of seven, at least. When my grandmother was left a widow at the age of 24, it was her brothers and brothers-in-law that supported her and her three infant children.

There is something almost instinctual about including others in our personal support system, especially if our natural families are distant, either by geography or emotion. In time, for many of us, our clubs, munches, and some of the folks at our favorite play parties become a kind of family. For some of us they become primary family and we begin to name them as such.

My own promiscuous activity is aimed as much as creating family as it is in getting laid. More than one slave wannabe has written about being "in your family." Certainly hundreds of Leather men talk about their partners, lovers, slaves, and boys as "their family." Likewise there is an increasing number of Het players who look at polyamory as family, unique and far from what the Cleavers and Nelsons may have looked like, but every way as supportive. It was expected, then, that when Master Lynn's lover John passed away in 2004, that I would spend a few days with him in the early days of his grief, that I would call him weekly, invite him to join us for weekends, and in any way possible be there as family. "Expected?" Yes, I expected to do those tasks because they (John and Lynn) were (and remain) part of our family.

When my friend Donna (who lived in San Antonio) told me of her diagnosis of terminal cancer, it was natural for Patrick and me to find time to visit her and to offer our home as her place to live, if living alone were no longer an option. She was part of our family, and family supports, comforts, tends to, and cares for its members. It's not that we come to kink expecting that the ties that bind be other than rope, leather, or chain, but that often happens.

Like all human relationships, Leather family grows organically. Though it is often desired and actively sought, it develops only slowly, friend by friend. It takes time for familiarity to become family and for family to become strong.

Most families, too, have a wide variety of "members." Differences of geography, intensity, sexual activity, hierarchy, frequency, dependability, and intimacy come to mind. So, for instance, David is part of our family. He lives in Chicago and we see him about once a month -- at meetings or parties. He is a regular invitee for holiday meals. We are close friends but not sexually intimate.

Joel, on the other hand, lives in Philadelphia and makes it a point to visit us three or more times a year. He and I talk on the phone at least weekly and he also talks to Patrick on about the same schedule. We enjoy an on-going, if infrequent, love affair, sexual contact, even at a rather great distance.

My former master, Lynn, is the closest "extended" family member -- he lives north of Chicago and is often an overnight guest in our home. In this case, "our" includes him, as we consider him a close member of our household and no guest, even if he does have his own home in the northern suburbs. He and I no longer have sexual intimacy, but he knows he is free to use Patrick when he wishes, which is rarely.

Donna, mentioned above, was not sexually intimate with me but our friendship spans more than 20 years. In this case she was more "my family" than family to Lynn, David, or Joel. There are others, of course, who are less close but still family. And family includes other family as well, since I do have two children, parents, a son-in-law and two grandsons. Indeed, it is a beautiful collage of friends and lovers, each bringing something to the lives of the others, in various kind and different degrees.

There is no secret to creating family. You start with a person whom you like and you befriend them. That means you treat them like a friend. Want to make a friend? Then be a friend. There is no mystery, no complexity. What it does take, though, is your effort: your reaching out to others by extending friendship and letting it develop as best it can. Sure, it doesn't work with everyone. Yes, it means taking a risk, making yourself available, vulnerable, and helpful.

I've found friends at parties, at bars, online, through other friends, at conventions, at school, at church, and in many other ways as well. What is common in all of these "findings" is that each of us had to take some kind of small risk -- saying hello, inviting the other to dinner, volunteering to help and then doing so. You've got to give the other person a reason to befriend you in return and that means taking a risk, extending your hand and yourself.

It also means accepting them where they are, meeting them more than half-way, and making an effort. It means turning off the television and getting off the couch in order to listen, share, and extend yourself to the other. Only by first reaching out will you find those who will reach back. It doesn't always work, of course, but when it does, the effort is well worth it.

Daddies and Sirs

September 8, 1992

There used to be a story that went around about an editor, finding himself older, greyer, and less in demand, who started to publish stories of older men and their "boys." The idea caught on and Daddies became as popular as the "pretty boys of GQ." Such may be the case, but I suspect that there has always been an interest in Daddy. After all Socrates certainly appreciated his share of younger sex partners!

The relatively recent rise in Sir and Boy contests illustrates how wide a demand there is. It also shows how innovative we can be in creating new social patterns. That said, let the "moral majority" take note. We love family as much as anyone and "We are family" is more than a line in a hit song, because we work at making family happen.

During these contests, men (and women, since in our culture both daddy and boy are gender non-specific) present themselves as Daddies and each of them often has a different perspective on what that means. Consistent in each answer, though, is a strong sense of caring. Mentor, disciplinarian, director, friend, are just some of the names that Dads use to describe themselves.

It is interesting to hear these "guys" talk about their "boys". There is an unmistakable thread about discipline. In fact, sometimes it isn't easy to see where most of them draw the line between "boy" and "slave;" hence the confusion that arises between those two terms.

Repeatedly, there is the reminder that the "passing down" of experience is a number one priority in the Daddy/Boy relationship. "I've been there before and I can help him avoid the trouble I had," is echoed by more than one Dad.

I don't answer the way many Dads do. That makes it clear that my opinions aren't always shared by the rest of the Leather community. And therein lies the beauty of Leather folk. We don't agree and don't have to. We are free to explore our own relationships and define them as best suits us and our partners.

I used to have a boy named Jim. He didn't want me to whip him and I didn't. Other boys crave the "attention" of a whip. What matters is that the relationship between Dad/Mom and Son/

109

Girl satisfies the men and women in that particular relationship. And it is just that: two people relating for reasons personally defined and meaningful to their authentic selves.

Of course we each have images of what a Dad is. They often have the typical Dad look: dark beard with grey, dressed in Leather from head to toe, muscled or hunky, relatively trim (but not always), self-assured. They are what any gay Leather boy might want to become. Please note that my female readers might want to substitute their own fantasy Dad into this picture.

That of course is the benefit of having Daddies in our midst. They provide role models, proof that the Gay and/or kinky life can be the strong masculine, winningly good life. Young, uncertain, untried as we may be, we can survive. Beaten, ridiculed and rejected, we can prosper.

Not all Daddies fit the role of Dominant either. I know my share of older, greyer men who are slave daddies. It is their boys who wield the discipline, their sons who lead them. I used to know a successful Michigan business manager, handsome, educated and well-paid in his government job, who was a "slave" to a younger man here in Chicago. The Dad boasted of his love and service to his Master, a man at least ten years younger than he.

What makes the Leather scene controversial is its iconoclastic behavior. Younger Dad and older son. Man with man or woman with woman creating family. Icon crashing at its best. In the idea of Daddy and boy there is the scent of lechery, of incest, of complete generational confusion.

I once met a very handsome, blond kid at Deeks (a Chicago bar), named "K B", the kind of young guy anyone would want to know. Cute, sparking eyes, trim 'stache, impish look about him. After we talked a while it became obvious that nothing would happen without Dad's permission.

As it turned out "Dad" was a Lesbian. K B was a lesbian as well. She was out for a good time, exploring the masculine side of her life. I later talked with K B at a SM University seminar. This time she was decked out in full Leather, sans 'stache. Obviously, now that I knew her, she was a woman of Leather. Her comments were well thought out as she reflected on gender roles, models, stereotypes, and the exploration of self.

It was the experience of living all sorts of lives that attracted her to Leather, of realizing the many selves that she could become. Her Daddy was strong and reliable and the title "Daddy" wasn't based on sexual identity but on role. She had overcome gender-restricted values to see the wider meaning of relationship.

Leather really is the freedom to be who you are and the responsibility to allow others to be themselves as well. I used to love being "Dad" and Jim let me do it, on terms that brought each of us closer to our own selfhood.

Father's Day was special then for several reasons. One of them was that the love that my boy gave me enriched my life.

The friendship, the laughs, the companionship, and the reasons to shake my head in disbelief, made knowing him, and having him as son, a wonderful experience. In a concise sentence, a richer, fuller life is what he gave me and that is what the Leather quest is all about.

Change

August 02, 2006

Father Alliot always said (in French) that "The more things change, the more they stay the same." He was an elderly priest whom I knew during my seminary years. A wise man, to be sure. Change is always with us. In fact, change is our only constant.

I have a large jar on the floor in my bedroom and I often put whatever coins I have in my pocket into it. It's another kind of change but illustrative of change in general. You see, each day (if I've gotten some change) as little as a penny or much as four quarters gets stashed there. In any case it's not much and I don't miss it. Over time, though, those few coins add up and I eventually bring them to the bank. It is then that the change has become significant, perhaps adding up to sixty or seventy dollars. Change is like that, especially in relationships. We don't often notice the little changes that occur daily. I see it with my folks. From visit to visit they are only a little different. From decade to decade they have become completely different people.

At dinner time I see a painting of my mother hanging on the wall. Painted in 1944, she is an attractive woman full of life and potential. At age 87, she is a quiet old crone, mostly senile and very fragile. Years of change have marked her, re-formed her, as they do all of us.

Dealing with change isn't easy. It's often because we don't even see it to deal with it. It is so subtle, sneaking up on us in the smallest amounts that we often miss it entirely. Eventually, though, there is something that exposes the cumulative effect of change to our sight, and we don't know what to do. That which was so comfortable, so familiar has become strange and unsettling. There was a transformation right under our noses and we smelled it not.

The other day I read this post on a newsgroup, edited greatly to protect anonymity: "After six years in my service, slave has begged for release." How painful it must have been to write those words. What dreams were dashed, what comfort lost? What changes took place under master's nose or in slave's feelings that grew silently and unknown?

Coping with change is difficult because the status quo has

its own form of comfort. It is known. We have lived with its pattern and so know what to do. A new pattern confronts us with the unknown, bringing doubt and fear into our lives. "How has he changed? Does he still love me?" we ask ourselves. "What went wrong?" we question, seeking answers that we cannot find. We search in agony and futility for the hints and clues, the tell-tale residue that might show us the change that we missed seeing while it was occurring.

"If I had only known," we sigh. "Why didn't you tell me?" we plead. "What could I have done to prevent it?" we wonder. Like the two or three coins a day, we thought not much of the change at all. We added it to the pile of our lives in such small amounts that we missed seeing the pile grow. As with a stack of straw, we never thought that one little piece of straw would be noticed, until it was the one that broke the camel's back.

That's not to say that change is for the worse. I think of Patrick and me and how different we are. When we met in 1996, I was a collared slave with a lover. I seldom traveled, had only had one book in print, and lived in a small condo. Patrick came to me as a very quiet man, who was careful not to disturb the status quo. Ten years later, the collar has been long off me, and I have a national reputation. We own the home in which we live, the lover has long gone to another love in another state, and Patrick and I are partnered with Matthew as well.

For his part, Patrick is much more his own man, confident in his profession, known and admired in his own right, and more devoted to me than ever. Simply put we have both grown for the better. The changes have been good.

Good, yes, but not always easy. I agonized for months over my break-up with the lover. Master Lynn was badly pained by my request to have the collar removed. Today's success was built on struggle and fear of loss. Sometimes life was so stretched that I had to grab coins out of that jar just to get to work. There have been illnesses, elderly parents with whom to deal, difficulties in our relationships which we had to negotiate, arguments and hurts that we had to heal.

And always we had to face change. At times it has snuck up on us. At other times it was more obvious but still held no easy solution for coping with it. It is one thing to simply remove a collar or a wedding ring, another to figure out "What do we do now?" The transition from Lynn's slave to Lynn's friend was not easy but over time it was managed successfully and with great results.

Our friend John, who became Lynn's slave after me and then became his lover, died two years ago, another change for us to painfully face. As John's death illustrates, change is often out of our control. John died on the operating table and the doctor struggled to bring him back, but it was not to be. Change kills more than friends. It kills hopes and dreams and plans and expectations. It seems to rob us of the very future that guided our lives and gave us hope.

The pain of change makes it difficult to discuss it. The fact of change fills us with disappointment, with anger, and especially with the loss of what we once knew surely would be. Change teaches us that there is no "surely," no certainty, no security. Is there anything as important as security? To know that we are safe in this relationship, that our future is assured, that there is no danger because the future (we foolishly think) is known. And then it isn't known. It becomes dark, foreboding, and impossible to face because that which we thought we knew is gone, replaced by questions with no easy answers because there are no facts about the future upon which we can rely.

So we are left with the only choice that makes sense: to embrace the present, to acknowledge what is and to love it, live it, to be in the moment, knowing that change is our only constant. By living in the now, enjoying what we have is the only way to find security. Not an easy proposition but what else is there? That said, I wish the master and his un-collared slave peace and security in the present and love to carry them into the future.

More on Change

August 09, 2006

If change is always with us and change affects our relationships, then it is necessary that we find ways to deal with it. That, of course, is easier written than done. Both the people of whom I wrote in the previous essay (anonymously) recognized themselves and wrote to me. One partner told me one side of the story, the other noted that they had changed and wanted to repair the relationship. I invited both of them to contact me via phone, as there are times when typing just won't work.

OK, what happens now?

First off, if they call me or you, remind them that we are not professional counselors and that our advice is worth what they are paying for it, namely nothing. None of us, and unfortunately this includes professional therapists and relationship counselors, can really tell another person what to do. We can only tell them what we think we would do given the circumstances as we see them. Remember, folks, that we're not walking in their moccasins nor looking at the world through their eyes. Perception is everything and no two of us perceive in the same way, even if it appears to be the same event we are perceiving.

If you are lucky enough to be reading this column knowing that your Relationship is healthy and solid, remember that relationships most often are spelled with a lower case "r." All relationships are subject to change, even if it's only the hands on the clock that are changing.

Time is both our friend and our foe. The best advice begins with the admonishment to take it slowly. Speak slowly, plan slowly, react slowly, move slowly. If you let yourselves get caught up in the frenzy of the moment, change will carry you along in a rapid and uncontrollable way, often leaving you at a regrettable point of no return. Time is our foe because it is the author of most change. It is our friend because eventually it will reveal all, and because if we take our time, our decisions will be more reliable. Of course, time's telling is not on our own timetable, so be careful about holding your breath while waiting to find the answer.

If the threat to your relationship seems significant to you, **115** then seeking the counsel of a competent third party, if only to facilitate your dialogue, is probably a good idea. Unfortunately, nearly every "family counselor" I've ever seen has watched over the end of that relationship. Honestly, though, I think it is safe to say that my partner and I only sought counseling when the relationship was long past restoring. For that reason, earlier rather than later intervention can be helpful. Yes, finding a kink-friendly counselor may prove quite the challenge but I dare say it is not impossible. As Mom says, "Where there is a will there is a way."

As you may have noted in my comment about the failure of counseling, there is much to be said about the role of preventative maintenance. Have you and your partner(s) found a way to cope with change before it hits one or both of you in the face? Change, as I noted last week, may creep up on you silently, but that's no reason for you not to be ready for it. It is, after all, inevitable and therefore can hardly be called unexpected.

Healthy dialogue is the best kind of prevention, but then we have to know how to communicate with one another. Listening skills are often not what we would want them to be. Neither are, for that matter, speaking skills. So even our words can work against us. Added to the problems of meaning and interpretation are the problems of feelings. Is what you say based on fact or feeling? Is it what it is or what you think it is? In polyamorous relationships the difficulty of communication is seriously compounded by "he said" and "she said" sentences, where communication can get really screwed up as what one repeats is filtered by what one thinks they heard and the agendas they have when they repeated it.

What then are our options? How can we grow while preserving the very relationships that foster our growth?

First off, each of us has to know and live according to our priorities, the first one of which needs to be authenticity. Too often we are willing to compromise some part of ourselves in order to "get what we want." Yes, compromise is necessary, but the very act of compromise may in fact destroy authenticity, thereby sowing the seeds of destruction. I am as guilty of that as anyone else. Too often I choose silence (don't we all?) in order to maintain peace in the house. But it is an uneasy peace that only lurks as a cover for an inner dissatisfaction, an unspoken frustration which becomes an inner anger, that, at some moment, will erupt into a not-so-silent expression of rage. It seems that silence is the easier route, but in the end it is the deadly one.

I have found that journaling is a good way to understand oneself, to keep track of the variations of one's feelings, of noting change so that one can be prepared to cope with it, of giving voice to those thoughts and feelings that are otherwise difficult to express. Likewise having a good friend listen can facilitate the same process. Understanding oneself ought to be easy, but unfortunately that is often not the case. In this, of course, we have to recognize that we are responsible for our lives and our decisions.

When it comes to relationships it is extremely easy to assume a victim role, blaming others for our failure to be authentic.

We need to make time to communicate. It will happen neither automatically nor quickly. It won't happen on the fly or in the midst of distraction. It is dangerous to do it in the "heat of the moment." The need for time means that the improvements won't and can't happen quickly. It often takes a long time to get ourselves into a relational morass. It is only reasonable, then, to accept that it will take a long time to get out of it. Problems that have had years to grow won't disappear with one good discussion or one quick agreement. Patterns that we have lived for years won't be different just because we say we want them to change. But change they can, given time, commitment, authenticity, and the work it takes to create positive change and to cope with all change. And change we will, which is why being proactive is always the better course. As Mom says, "A stitch in time saves nine."

Passion

August 18, 2006

My previous two essays on change omitted any consideration of passion, one of the most important aspects of change. I write this because change is often a catalyst for the expression of quite a bit of passion. Calling it passion belies its other, more common name, emotion.

I realize that my recent essays might give the idea that I'm more a "Dear Abby" than a columnist writing about kinky sex. More realistically, though, for better or for worse, emotion is very much part of many scenes. Sex of any kind alters one's feelings; alternative sexual practices hold the potential to alter our feelings even more.

One of the important values of Leathersex is that it offers the time and place to express one's emotions in a safe and controlled environment. If you've ever seen a guy bound to a St Andrew's cross while being intensely flogged, you know what I mean. There's a good chance that he is screaming, yelling, and flailing about, expressing all kinds of emotions of a rather loud and powerful nature. The bondage that keeps him on the cross protects both him and his flogging partner from gyrating into danger. The consensual nature of the scene allows him to rant and rave himself into blissful oblivion, releasing his pent-up passion in an environment that allows such actions without fear of reprisal or injury.

In themselves emotions are neutral in value, neither good nor bad. Too often we fail to remember that emotions are necessary as they encourage us toward the good, such as when we "feel" love, and they impel us from the bad, such as when fear drives us to flee from danger. Unfortunately we seldom deal with emotions in a neutral environment. Instead emotion is felt within the context of widely varying forces in which they are able to overpower reason and safety so that we act, or more correctly react, on the basis of emotion only, forsaking all other rationales and becoming so passionate as to become unbalanced and therefore less human.

This too happens in the dungeon, as when fear grips the man on the cross and he becomes hysterical. I once had this experience with a slave applicant. He was tied rather tightly next to my bed, a position he had seemed to desire. All of a sudden the reality of his immobility hit him full force and he panicked, becoming somewhat uncontrolled within the confines of the ropes and chains. I had to gently talk him down from his raging fear while releasing him from the restraints.

When he was both released and calmed he wanted to return to that bondage, something that I felt he should do only once he realized how his emotions had overpowered the scene and he understood what had happened, so that he could prevent its reoccurrence. In subsequent play he was often restrained even more forcefully than during this scene, but fortunately he had learned to "subdue his passion" in order to enjoy the bondage.

I use the Masonic phrase "subdue his passion" in order to be clear as to the place and nature of controlling and expressing one's feelings. It is of the utmost importance that we find the balance between repression of feelings and allowing feelings to uncontrollably rule us. It is for that reason that I wrote that emotions are neutral, since they can be used for good or for ill, depending upon their role in our decisions and activities.

During the late sixties and early seventies, for instance, I was angry about the Vietnamese War. As did many Americans, I had a real choice as to how I could express that anger. I could protest in destructive rage or I could work constructively to change the political climate of my country. We are often confronted with such choices, even if they are not as global as war. The question is always one of "How shall I deal with this feeling?" That question always arises because feelings will not be denied. They are real and have a real effect on us and our actions, even if we attempt to deceive ourselves that we don't feel a certain way or that the feelings have no effect on us and those around us.

To be sure, there are times when our feelings are unclear. We don't know what we feel or why. The feeling may be no more than a lingering twinge, a slight discomfort. It may be unconsciously repressed or hidden by thoughts and/or habits. Many of us, after all, have been taught not to feel or that certain feelings are evil and need to be denied. SM, on the other hand, offers the opportunity to feel and emote those feelings in a safe and controlled environment. Negotiated limits allow us to explore fear, rage, lust, and anger while both our partner and the scene which we mutually create protect us from damage and destruction. After all, sometimes a good cry is just what we need and there is nothing like a good flogging to release us so that we can cry.

In any discussion about emotions and BDSM, the notion of negotiated limits is important. Though scenes can be cathartic, they ought not be seen as therapeutic. By that I mean that we can certainly find emotional release through SM activity, but that we ought to strictly avoid playing therapist or patient when we do so. When scenes begin to show us areas where psychological help is needed, we ought to bring those experiences to the counsel of those competent to guide us through them to healing.

In other words, most emotional trauma cannot be resolved simply with the use of emotional release. Release is an important component of healing but it must be accompanied by self-understanding, forgiveness, and acceptance of the healing processes that might be necessary to resolve them. In that regard expression of an emotion during a scene becomes an indication that work may be needed, not that it is being done.

Several years ago, for instance, I was faced on several occasions with Patrick's angry reaction to what I was doing while we were having sex. He became angry with me, expressed the anger and in a rage left the bedroom, slamming the door behind him. Although in every instance he soon returned in a composed state, the anger was a clear indication that something was amiss. It took several months of discussion outside of both the dungeon and the bedroom before we could resolve our problem. His anger, after all, wasn't only his, but I had to recognize my part in creating, sustaining, and eventually resolving it.

There certainly isn't enough space here to delve into the processes of arriving at balance. I can only encourage you to find ways to reach it on your own or with competent counsel.

Dealing With Emotions

July 12, 1998

If having experience is any criterion, I'm the perfect person to write this essay. First off, I usually wear my heart on my sleeve. I find it difficult, if not impossible, to hide my feelings. I've been told, of course, that I should. I even had one memorable phone conversation with my Dad who said, "If you don't stop crying right this minute, I'm going to hang up on you." Those words came from a man whom I have never seen cry. I feel sorry for him about that, but it is his life, not mine. He is living in the context of his own life and upbringing – at least it shows that I wasn't raised with a father role-model who wore his heart on his sleeve!

Secondly, my emotions carry me on rather frequent roller-coaster rides. I go from high to low and back to high in no time at all. Thirdly, there have been days, weeks, and even months when depression was all that really affected me. Yes, I've considered suicide.

I tell friends that the only reason I'm not dead is that I didn't own a garage. A guy whom I dated when I first came out asphyxiated himself with the exhaust from his car as it was parked in his closed garage. He took care to make all his arrangements, left messages for friends (myself included) and sat in the car until the undertaker carried him away. So I know it can be done and no, I'm not going to try doing it. That is one way to deal with one's feelings – though my doctor would be quick to point out that there are other, less drastic solutions.

What else can I tell you?

I can tell you that I've had rabid arguments, spates of joy, times of excitement. I am familiar with doldrums, with pleasure, with contentment. I can add, too, that emotions are only one factor in the equation called life.

So why this essay? I've been thinking specifically about what I should write since 9 am. Nine hours later I am still at a loss. Why? Because I have all sorts of feelings coursing through my mind and they overshadow all the ideas, possibilities, and topics that you might have read if I hadn't been so pre-occupied with how I feel.

121

The truth is, of course, that I am really "well" in many ways.

Those of you who have been reading regularly for the last few months know all the good things that are going on in my life. Things are going well, very well. But I can still wake up in the morning and feel like I don't want to write a column, much less get out of bed. What does this have to do with Leather? "Plenty," Jack said.

Sex, kinky or otherwise, is all about relationships – and how we feel very often determines how well or how poorly the relationship goes.

Take the e-mail from a recent slave-applicant: "It seems that discussion of slavery and a future as such puts me in a mind-set that makes it difficult for me to focus on my day-to-day life here. It's a struggle to balance it for me right now, as I have had several personal interactions this week that have left me reeling and saddened." That was in response to some e-mail I sent because I was upset that the guy had missed a date to chat with me on-line.

As it turns out, he missed the agreed upon time because he fell asleep. I tried five times unsuccessfully to get a hold of him. Failing to do so depressed me. All of a sudden I was thinking the guy was jerking me around, irresponsible, and uncaring. My emotions took the opportunity to give me a perspective that made me feel bad over an incident that was completely un-noteworthy. Get my point?

The operative word here is perspective. How do you deal with emotions? Find a way to put them into perspective. OK, sometimes that's easier said than done. Sometimes it only takes a nap, a conversation with a friend, a walk along the lake.

I find that writing helps. If you've never done any journaling you might try it just to put your thoughts in order.

Those people who have a hard time deciding about something (such as whether they want to make a commitment) ought to keep a diary of their daily feelings. Today may be a "Yes," tomorrow a definite "No." After some time, add the pluses and minuses and see how you've felt over the long haul. Another use of paper and pen is to compare the emotional responses to the intellectual, physical, financial, social, moral, legal, and ethical ones. Does what you understand about life support your feelings or contradict it? Expressing your feelings on paper also lets you see them in a different light.

An applicant once wrote that he wants to be subdued, even though he admits that he's not a submissive. Such feelings may quite well be very valid – real as feelings, but not very real in terms of practicality. Exploring such feelings, though, can lead to a deeper understanding of more fundamental emotions.

It turns out (and here I am playing amateur psychiatrist) that he is rather troubled by some paranormal events in his life. It's my opinion (admittedly not worth much) that he's not so much looking to be controlled as to find some way to control the psychic experiences that haunt him. I'm not saying that a relationship won't help. I'm only saying that there is more here than meets the eye. That, of course, is most often the case with us humans.

Emotions come into play during sex, too. If you've never had a bottom get angry at you or if you've never lost your temper at your partner, then you must be real new to getting it on with another person.

It's best, when emotions create an uncomfortable situation, to recognize what is happening and to deal with it in an non-emotional way. Most of the time, of course, feelings will pass quickly. I'm not suggesting that dungeons be used for therapy --- in fact I'm rather opposed to using them that way, but the intensity of a scene can, and will, bring up all sorts of unexpected emotions. Pause to recognize them and deal with them accordingly. "Dealing" may consist of something as easy as taking a deep breath or as significant as ending the scene.

In either case, ignoring what has happened, in the long run, may not be very healthy. In the short run, it may be the only realistic alternative. In spite of what my Dad might think, there's nothing wrong about expressing our emotions. Use them as a guide. Explore them to better know yourself. Analyze them to better understand the full implications of what's going on. To be sure, they are important. The trick is to keep them in perspective.

Emotions, Again

August 04, 2002

There are a great many ways in which we can discuss the topic of emotions as they pertain to SM activity: top, bottom, controlled, chaotic, wanted, denied, and repressed are only a few. I'm certainly not able to cover the full range here, but it won't hurt to briefly discuss some of the pertinent issues.

It is natural that the top's administration of pain and pleasure is going to arouse his or her bottom emotionally. Their reactions to this will vary: some tops enjoy witnessing emotions while others prefer their partners to "hang tough." Likewise some bottoms use SM to release their emotions; others prefer to show their metal, so to speak, by exhibiting stoic silence. What is certain is that there is no one way that is the right way, though there are circumstances that may affect each action.

Noise, for instance, might be a factor. We don't need to have the neighbors calling the police because they heard someone screaming bloody murder, even when doing so is cathartic, even pleasant, for those involved. I love to hear the groans that Patrick gives forth as I squeeze my fingernails into his scrotum. It is, after all, a sure way to make me cum, but if the people downstairs or across the hall heard him, it probably wouldn't have the same effect on them.

I remember with fondness the times when Master Lynn applied crops, paddles, and floggers to my backside. I tended to keep to the quiet side. For me it was a matter of "proving myself." At times, though, I did experience the catharsis of tears, such as once while he was taking some fifty clothespins off my chest and genitals.

Because we all have control issues, emoting may or may not be a welcome event. Some, for instance, may think that expressing oneself in screams, tears, or rage is exactly the correct reaction, while others feel the opposite. Everyone is entitled to their scene, so we'll leave the final conclusion to those doing the doing. It's a good idea for first time partners to have some idea of the latitude of possible emotions that may arise. In public scenes, it is often helpful, sometimes even necessary, to inform the dungeon master as well. He or she will be glad to have been forewarned.

On the other hand, care must be taken that the use of emotions be balanced with intellect, safety, and care. On occasion it is quite possible that you will experience, either in yourself or from your partner, an expression of emotion that is quite overwhelming. I remember just such an event in my dungeon in Ft. Wayne many years ago.

A fisting bottom from Chicago had come down to play for the weekend. We had had a good time on the mattress where I had fisted him and were taking a short break before we returned to our playing. It was then that I casually asked him how he had gotten involved in the Leather scene. What followed was an incredible story of a child who had been deserted by his father before his birth, passed from relative to relative until he ended up in an orphanage, where an older boy became his "protector" in return for sexual favors.

We were obviously sharing intimacies in a different, though not uncommon, way. Eventually we returned to playing. Once again we became fully aroused and I took advantage of his well-opened ass hole. As I shoved my dick in and out of him, he began crying. As tears streamed down his face he sobbed, "Fuck me, Daddy. Fuck me." Our scene had gotten him in touch with his unhappy past and the lost boy in him was crying out. For him it was cathartic, cleansing. For me it was a complete surprise.

It's at a time like this that it is important to keep your partner balanced, allowing him or her their space to emote while you support them with peaceful, nurturing care. It's also important that we realize that neither the bedroom nor the dungeon is an appropriate place for therapy. It is quite all right to be a friend, but not a psychiatrist in this kind of situation.

Whether a scene is emotionally charged or not, it's always a good idea to take time together to "come down" from the high of playing. Relax quietly with your partner and make sure that both of you have balanced, centered, and calmed yourselves. It's also a good idea to check in with each other later, perhaps the next day, to assure one another that there wasn't any unpleasant aftermath, often called top- or bottom-drop.

Scenes aren't the only places where you'll experience emotions. We are, after all, a human subculture and there will be more times than we wish to count that unwelcome emotions will rear their heads. You'll find in our very human midst jealousy, anger, fear, and confusion. At these times it's simply necessary to recognize the situation for what it is and use your best skills to defuse it.

Emotions are a significant part of being human. We may want to think of ourselves as "rational," but in fact our reasoning is often based as much on feeling as on fact or logic. There is nothing wrong with this. In fact, to live otherwise is to be just as unbalanced.

125

Confusion and Conflict

November 30, 2006

Once again I received inspiration from the people who came into my life. Last week there were two who pointed my thoughts in the same direction. The first was David, who came for a weekend visit. Originally he had sent me a slave application but after discussing his goals and experience level with him I advised him that petitioning for slavery was premature since he needed more experience before he could really come to such a decision. The second voice of inspiration came in the form of an email from a perennial wannabe (I'll call him Steve) who has even less experience than David. In both cases they share a lack of experience and feel confused.

According to my trusty Webster Seventh Collegiate Dictionary, confusion is "the quality or state of being confused." Not much help there until we see that confused means perplexed and that to confuse means to make indistinct, to blur; to mix indiscriminately, jumble; to mistake for another.

As I lay in bed with David on the last morning of his visit, he admitted to being confused. It was then that I suggested that he was not so much confused as conflicted, an "emotional tension resulting from incompatible inner needs or drives."

I've been saying for years that we need to give newbies a dictionary when they join our subculture. As may be obvious from the above vocabulary lesson, confusion, that over-used explanation for doing nothing, is dispelled by experiences that bring clarity. Folks who are confused, I think, simply don't have enough facts to see the problem, the situation, or the opportunity clearly enough to discern how they should act.

Let me cite Steve's email: "Thank you for the advice. I am probably not the first person that you have counseled who is so drawn as a submissive to serve a Master, yet also struggling with what boundaries and lines to draw. I hope someday to meet you and have the slave part of me trained by you. Does my being drawn to serve a male master mean I am Gay? [I ask] because I am not drawn to living in a Gay world. It seems to be more about the SM that I am drawn to. I am also still attracted to women."

Facts, Steve, facts. Learn what it means to be bisexual.

Understand that there are alternatives on the Kinsey scale between hard core Het and hundred percent Queer. Any amount of experience in the scene will show you that. Get the facts. Any time spent with a Gay man will show that none of us live in a Gay world. As I wrote back to him: "I am Gay. I occasionally find a woman attractive. I have two children. Yes, I am out and well-known as a Gay man, but that does not mean I live in a Gay world. I live in a human one. Am I Gay when I teach at Columbia College? No more Gay than my straight colleagues are hetero in the classroom."

The sad fact is that Steve's inner conflicts are based on a great deal of misinformation. He erroneously thinks that being Gay means that you always and everywhere act in a homosexual way. There is nothing further from the truth. There's nothing queer about the way I shop at Costco, ride the subway, or teach computer science. I sleep, shower, and mow the lawn in the same way as any heterosexual man or woman I know.

David's conflicts are of a similar nature. I am sure he fears the loss of family, of income, of his hard-earned retirement funds. He fears he'll not be able to listen to his favorite music, attend concerts or the theater, or continue any of his usual habits and practices. These fears are based on a lack of information, especially the fear that he won't find a master who enjoys what he enjoys. Yet doing so will be, as we who have experience know, all part of the successful process.

The difficulty (I'd almost call it a tragedy) is that the confusion is used as a rationale to avoid getting experience, which is the cure for confusion. That experience can present a solution ought to be vibrantly clear. Instead confusion breeds fear, which often results in inaction.

Why do I advise getting experience? Because it brings answers. Any scientist who lacks information knows quite well that experimentation will give him or her the necessary experience to arrive at the answer, or at least indicate what's not the answer. It is exactly this "scientific model" that I suggest we use to dispel confusion and resolve inner conflict. Experimentation is not commitment. It is not a grand scale move into some irreversible process or state. It is not a "whole hog" plunge into the unknown. Instead it is "a tentative procedure or policy; an operation carried out under controlled conditions in order to discover an unknown effect or law, to test or establish a hypothesis, or to illustrate a known law; the process of testing."

I hope you see why I told David to get experience. It was only by doing so, "under controlled conditions," that he would learn whether or not his hypothesis (I want to be a slave) was correct or not. His experience ought not to have been a matter of quitting his job, selling his furniture, and moving in with some master. It was simply to spend a weekend in a limited D/s relationship. Because of his limited experience, I suggested that he not even try to act

127

the role of slave. Instead, he ought to find out if he was comfortable with the experience of bondage, spanking, and the other fetish activities that we kinky folks enjoy. Sure he fantasized about being flogged, but only experience would demonstrate whether or not he would actually enjoy the fantasy as it was being fulfilled.

Believe me. I have seen a great many players come to the realization that the fantasy was much better than the experience could ever be. The experience put the fantasy to rest forever. It was as simple as that.

There is a caveat necessary concerning the last paragraph. It is often the case that a little bit of experimentation "to get it out of my system" works the opposite effect. A taste of the forbidden only increases the desire for it. In either case, there are lessons to be learned in the experience, and that's the point of my essay.

Taking this experimental approach to ending inner turmoil or confusion removes the difficulty and demand to make a commitment or to become involved in ways that are premature. It is one thing to be flogged "for the experience" and another thing to be flogged as part and parcel of a committed relationship. The first is easy to accomplish; the second takes a long search for the right person to wield the flogger.

I will certainly grant you that the flogging by a partner can be of a higher quality than one done just "for the experience." But here I would then remind you that the whole idea is to learn through "a tentative procedure or policy; an operation carried out under controlled conditions." The idea is not to create the end result of the fantasy, which in this case would be committed 24/7 long term slavery to a master, but rather to gather enough information to know how to proceed in that direction and whether or not proceeding in that direction is the right direction.

It is this small-step approach that ends inner conflict and clears away confusion. I encourage you to take those small steps, as it is only by taking small steps that you will learn how to run with the wind.

Our Culture

The Cost of Fear

May 05, 2007

Threformer seminarian in me wants to remind you that Jesus is frequently quoted as saying "Fear not," after his resurrection. The point is, of course, that understanding and overcoming fear often comes only after we have conquered our fears by living through the trauma that we feared. Honestly, what we fear most seldom happens. If it does, it seldom happens the way we feared it would.

Denouncing fear is one of my favorite topics, but I realized this weekend that I have never written about the price we pay when we are afraid. We think that by giving in to our fear we are doing nothing, i.e., not doing that which we are afraid to do, and therefore there are no consequences. Since we don't experience the consequences of what we feared, we think our "risk-free" behavior has no effects. This is an illusion.

All actions have consequences. The law of causation is always in effect. That being so, fearing has its consequences, which for the sake of being literary I call the cost of fear.

I am not talking about discretion, reason, or doubt. Each of these provides a healthy and useful premise upon which to base our actions or inactions. I am talking, rather, about fear, "an unpleasant, often strong emotion caused by anticipation or awareness of danger." The operative principles here have to do with emotion and danger.

Is the fear simply an emotion? If so, then we have to look at the problem holistically and see how we evaluate it using reason, common sense, real data, and our personal values. What is the danger we fear and is it serious enough that it trumps other outcomes? What is the probability of the danger? Is it small or great? Even if great, is the possible or intended outcome worth the risk? That noted, let me comment on the cost of fear.

Sometimes the price we pay because we fear is silence. I would even go so far as to write the price we pay most often is silence. Think about the times when you kept your mouth shut because you feared that what you would say might change what people thought about you, how people acted towards you, or that it was "best" to leave well enough alone. You feared the consequences of your speech.

Would your speech have been honest? Truthful? Just? What a price we pay with silence. Silence can prolong injustice. It can continue suffering. It can sustain an unpleasant status quo.

Fear paralyzes. What great amount of constructive criticism, thoughtful advice, creative ideas, new approaches, strengthened support, and successful invention goes undone because we are afraid to act? Paralyzed, we do nothing. Nothing, on the other hand, still does something because we have decided not to decide. We have chosen the status quo.

Fear echoes. Our fear instills fear in others, multiplying its cost. Fear preserves and sustains dysfunctional relationships. How often are we afraid to talk honestly and openly with our partners, our lovers, our companions, or our significant others by whatever name we call them? Fear is the incubator in which small hurts are harbored and grow, added to over time by other small hurts until, as the straw is loaded upon the camel, one hurt, of no consequence in itself, is added to the load which breaks the back in two.

On a broader scope, fear destroys our communities. I am convinced that the bedrock of our subculture is composed of three values: Trust, Respect, and Honor. Certainly the lip service given these three would imply agreement. Fear destroys them all. The cost of fear is the loss of trust: "Assured reliance on the character, ability, strength, or truth of someone or on something; one in which confidence is placed." Or we might turn it around and admit that fear is confidence that someone or something will harm us. Either way, the price is high, destroying respect and honor as well.

Then we pay for fear with our freedom. Fear binds us so that we can no longer act freely, doing that which is natural to our authentic selves. I am no longer free to be me. Instead I create a false persona built by fear, an invention that hides the real me in order to project a protective image. Although the projection may divert superficial criticism, it also kills my authenticity and distorts my being, twisting it into a shape that torments me and those around me.

Fear forbids living in the moment, savoring and enjoying the present. That is another cost of fear as it drags us to continually fear the future, and live in an imaginary time not yet come.

Fear destroys transparency, building an opaque screen around us. We think we are safe within its walls, when in fact we have cut ourselves off from light and vision. The closets we build seem comfortable, even if their cost is freedom, mobility, and growth. Closets are cells, imprisoning us in walls of fear, hiding our real selves from real others.

Self-Acceptance is the victim of our fear, as we learn to loathe our authentic self in order to protect ourselves from that which we fear. Yet the price of that protection is self-destruction. The real you succumbs to the fear and becomes the fearful you, the hiding you, the pretend-in-order-to-be-safe you, which of course is no safety at all.

It is no safety because now you have lost integrity, having traded it for a sense of safety. But it is an illusory sense, since the fear is still there, threatening you with its shadow and imagined dangers, and extolling its price.

I trust you see why I write so often about overcoming fear. It is a cancer that kills, albeit slowly, quietly, and often secretly.

It need not, of course. As the seminarian in me knows, "The truth shall set you free." Mostly that means that the truth will set you free from fear, as it is fear that binds us most strongly. Afraid to tell the truth, afraid to approach that stranger, afraid to have that talk with our roommate, afraid of what will happen, afraid to be authentic.

I can not give you a prescription that will take you out of your fear. I can only tell you that your fear is a mere shadow. It looks like an impenetrable wall, an obstacle of infinite height and width, a gulf so deep it reaches the foundations of hell itself, but it is none of those. It is a fog through which you can walk without even getting wet, a darkness with light on the other side. It is even darkness in which every step, if only the next step, is lit. Take that one step and the next one will be lit for you.

It is, after all, better to take one step toward the light than to wither in the darkness; better to light one little candle than to curse because you cannot see.

Earning Your Leathers

August 29, 1999

If you press me to use an histori-
cal context, I have to admit that "I never earned my leathers." I can
try to excuse myself by saying that (1) I lived in a geographically
non-Leather neighborhood so I had no club members to initiate me
or (2) that I am so young (yeah, right) that the tradition had passed
into history when I came out in Leather.

Tradition has it that "in the good old days (the fifties)," men
were inducted into Leather after a period of trial and training. Everyone was expected to start on the bottom (literally), learn the
proper etiquette, show due respect, gain the group's trust, and
then, and only then, be accepted into the group with an initiation
ceremony. That meant your elders gave you your first vest, bent
you over a motorcycle and pissed all over you. I don't have any
videos or 8 mm movies to demonstrate the activity, but that's how
I've heard it was done. If anyone has a home movie of such an
event, please send it to The Leather Archives and Museum --- it
would be priceless! If anyone reading this actually "earned their
leathers" in some traditional fashion, I'd like to interview them for
the Archives as well.

When "a bisexual stone butch" wrote asking, "Though I understand in general, and agree with, the concept of earning one's
leather, how does one take the concept and move it into reality?
What is the process of earning one's leather?" I thought I'd try and
give an answer.

The first answer, I guess, goes back to my recent column on Leather Clubs. Join a club, participate in its activities, and
let its members bring you into the Leather family as they see fit.
Somewhere in the process you will find that you have "earned your
Leathers." It may be they have a formal ceremony or it may be less
ritualized yet equally meaningful. Either way, you'll eventually see
yourself as a Leather person and others will too.

My leathers were earned in a much less formal way,
though I hope that my readers still appreciate that I earned them
and, more importantly, deserve them.   So now, here's a little
biographical history. When I was divorced in 1983, I came out as

a Gay man and a Leather man in one fell swoop. I kind of had to.

After all, I was nearly 37 years old and being a "late bloomer," wanted to make up for lost time. My attraction to men was, and is, intricately interwoven with my desire for Leathersex. It was therefore no mistake that they went together.

I read the books, went to Leather bars whenever possible, tricked with men who were into Leather, and learned by asking, listening, thinking, and experimenting. I can't emphasize too strongly the importance of doing all of the above. If all you do is fantasize, or read, or talk, you'll never be anything more than a wannabe. Leatherfolk are action-oriented. You have to do things, because experience is the best teacher and you earn your Leathers by gaining experience.

The bestowal of Leather is the recognition that you are (1) part of the community and (2) experienced in the ways that community lives.

So I tricked my way through the early months of my coming out, a process that began well before my divorce, I might add, getting as much experience as I could. In truth, I was trying to figure it all out. I date my "earning" to a week I spent in Corpus Christi, Texas. I was there on business and took the opportunity to go to a particular Leather bar every night. And every night I went home with another leather man. One, I remember, was more novice than I. The day after we met, I went to a hardware store and bought him some rope and clothespins. That night we met again and I gave him his first toys.

Another night, I went home with some leather-clad stud who handcuffed me to his bed and then proceeded to try and fuck me. I found that very threatening and got angry with him. I remember vaguely that I was afraid he was going to rape me. After some protestation on my part, he undid the cuffs and I got dressed. I had had enough of him. At the front door he pleaded with me not to leave. I relented and we went back into his bedroom where I then proceeded to fuck him.

My last night in Corpus was a Saturday. I got to the bar early. It was rather empty so the bartender, Scott, whom I had watched all week, and I struck up a conversation. It seemed he had the early shift and wanted to have a "date" with me after he was done working. He was a hot-looking leatherman and I was happy to oblige. So about 8 p.m. he left the bar, went home (which was just upstairs), showered and came back to meet me twenty minutes later. We then got into my rental car and went dancing. Yes, in full Leather we went to a mixed disco on the other side of town.

We ordered beers and started dancing. While we were doing so, young straight boys stared at us and their dates giggled. After about three dances, Scott said he wanted to take me back to his place for sex. I refused because he was flagging[1] top, which

1 Flagging is the practice of wearing a signifying key or hankerchief in your

meant his keys were on his left side. In no time at all he took his keys and put them on the right. So much for the value of flagging. It was guys like him (and all of us really) who killed flagging. He then said something and I said "What?" three times until he realized that he had to end his sentence with the word, "Sir."

Needless to say, we got back in the car and drove to his place. As I sat in his living room I told him to get his toys. He came out with rope and such and we started to play. An hour later I was done. To this day I wish I knew his last name and had his phone number. He was some hot bottom. But the end of the story is the most important part.

When we were finished, he looked me straight in the eyes and told me what a good top I was, what a good Leatherman I was. Ever since that night I have considered myself a Leatherman. I "earned" my leathers in his living room. Later that summer, my friend Ron and I went to Florida. On the way, I accidentally left my leather jacket on a chair in the airport. While in Florida Ron bought me a new one because he thought I should have one. That, too, was a kind of earning of my leathers.

As I've been writing this, I've been thinking that I've earned my Leather twice. In the above telling, I earned them in real life. More than seven years ago I began writing this column. No one knew who Jack Rinella was. How could they, since it was (and is) a pen name? Jack has earned his Leathers (we hope), by writing every week, by being honest, helpful, and authoritative. People have noticed and so, seven years later, I have a good reputation. I earned that reputation by working hard, by being truthful, by asking, listening, and learning. Most importantly I earned that reputation by being trustworthy.

There was no ceremony in all this and there need be none. I'm proud to be a Leatherman and I am that because you all have bestowed that recognition on me and I thank you for it.

So, dear bisexual stone butch, ask, listen, learn, experience, and be trustworthy. Before you know it, someone, somewhere will let you know that you've earned your leathers.

back pocket. Right side denotes a preference for the bottom; left top. It has generally fallen into disuse, though more traditional players still use the practice.

I Don't Believe It

May 04, 2005

Talk about an email to set me off: "Humbly I come before Thee requesting details on how one would validate a Grand Master of a registered house. What precept be there for those outside of the house system whom it's suggested be in receipt of tutelage particularly that of a BDSM Master with submissive given direction by said Old Guard Grand Master? It's in respect of TOG [that] I seek validation as [a] concern of trickery seeps upon one's mind limiting focus and diligence within the dynamics of the triangulation. Respectfully, [Name Withheld]

"[P.S.] I am unable to speak freely as I can not divulge the details of a particular house at this point; however, if in any way shape or form you are able to give guidance I would be appreciative."

My response was rather terse: "As far as I can tell, anyone who talks about 'Grand Master' and 'house' is usually full of bullshit." That written, I guess you don't really have to read any more of this column, but I will keep writing for your possible edification.

It took me a while to figure out what "TOG" meant and I came to the conclusion that it means "The Old Guard." I have had the honor of knowing actual Old Guard players, if going back to 1948 makes one a member of the Old Guard. They, in turn, knew older Old Guard players, so I guess I'm in good company.

I write that in spite of the fact that I often get emails that say something like this one did: "The organizer of my local BDSM group says she likes you because you are 'Old Guard.'" I appreciate the compliment but am not sure it actually applies, especially since I don't think of myself in that way. The question about houses really revolves around the facts of history, not nomenclature.

I have searched high and low looking for "houses" in Europe and ancient traditions handed down through the generations. I have come up with nothing. NOTHING. Get my drift? The Old Guard wasn't what most people think it was, as reflected in this email: "Your last entry [on your website] dates 2002 on the subject Old Guard. I was wondering if you have learned any more about this mysterious order." As an aside, let me note that it's quite probable that the Old Guard would get quite a loud laugh at being called a "mysterious order."

Both topics "Houses of Europe" and "Old Guard" need historical study, not conjecture. Go online and buy out-of-print books about what it is that we do and you'll find little or no mention of centuries-long houses. Ask any presenter who's been teaching for more than five years and every one will tell you they've never found any validity in the idea of houses either.

Now I'm not saying that BDSM is anything new. It's not. The walls of Pompeii are decorated with murals of sadomasochistic activity. There's nothing innovative about kinky sex. As best I can tell, the term "House" is used by those trying to validate themselves because they have no other way of appearing credible. Yes, I have friends who call their familial relationship a house, but none make a pretense of being ancient, descended from Europe, or to being (ugh) "Euro-trained."

Look at it in terms of simple logic. If the houses exist, then why don't we know of them? Why are they always spoken of in terms of one's being "unable to speak freely as I can not divulge the details of a particular house at this point?" I would posit that the reason is that there are no details to reveal. There is no time, no place, no actual participants who can testify to their reality. If, on the other hand, they exist and are clandestine, then one must posit that no "Master of a House" is going to expose him or herself on the Internet. One does not, after all, keep a secret by publishing it.

There is literature that we can research and what I've read is conspicuous in the absence of mention of old houses. A good example is "House of Pain" by Monique Von Cleef (1965), a celebrated mistress who began her practice at the end of World War II. Rob Bienvenue's dissertation, "The Development of Sadomasochism as a Cultural Style in the Twentieth-Century United States," is another excellent source. (See his website at http://americanfetish.net/)

It's way past time to cease all this idle speculation about our past. We can't afford to define terms as this writer does: "The term 'Old Guard' to me means one had the bravery it took for one to shake the fear of discovery to actually show up at an event." Definitions fail when they depend upon phrases such as "to me." Our vocabulary must have mutually agreed upon definitions or there will never be clear communication.

Look further at the "definition" and it reveals its lack of historical accuracy with the phrase "actually show up at an event." Yes, there have always been SM events, though they were more likely called "parties" than "events." In any case, one would never had been able to simply "show up," as if it were held in a Denny's or a Ramada Inn. Attendance at parties was by private invitation of those who had already been vetted by the host or someone well-known to the host. They were held in private homes, hidden (and likewise private) play spaces, or in remote mountain lodges and retreats. (See Viola Johnson's *To Love, to Obey, to Serve: Diary of an Old Guard Slave* for more details.)

Simply projecting today's methodologies backward in time is no way to define historical persons and events. Want to know about the Old Guard? Pick up a copy of Larry Townsend's original "Leatherman's Handbook." (1972) Buy a copy of Roger Earl's 1975 video "Born to Raise Hell." (available at www.bijou-world.com) or rent a copy of "The Wild One" with Marlon Brando (1953). Both videos give insight into what our Gay Old Guard was really like. After all, they were more akin to an unruly motorcycle gang than to a "mysterious order."

Even using the term Old Guard poses problems. Which Old Guard? The het one or the gay one? Though there seems to be a tendency to consider the Old Guard as the forefathers of Gay Leathermen, certainly the BDSM Het community has fore-parents as well. Even at that, it is well-known that the east coast Gay Old Guard differed from the west coast Old Guard in details, although not in values.

So a question such as "The reason I am writing to you this morning is that I received an email from someone asking me for information on what would be viewed as high protocol D/s," misses the mark. We are talking about very individualistic play-ers when it comes to D/s. One's high protocol probably differed a great deal from another's. As far as I can tell, in the Het commu-nity, the best resource for "high protocol" would have been Emily Post's "Book of Etiquette" (1922). The Gay community probably reflected a more military-like perspective, especially after World War II.

In the end, specifics such as protocols probably don't mean anywhere near as much as the values that they represent. It is the values of the Old Guard, such as trust, honor, and respect, that are important. It is qualities such as those that created our subculture(s), not frivolous guessing about what might have been. Ask that Old Guard Grand Master for references and I'll bet there are none. Without verifiable references, I'm not gong to believe him and neither should you. That is, after all, the Old Guard way of doing things. As for me, "References available upon request."

Two Attitudes

October 14, 2005

This email reflects a list of common questions: "What is Old Guard? What is New Guard? Which is stricter? Which are you, if any? I just don't get the whole new/old thing, can you explain the difference, Sir?"

I'm going to let others debate the meaning of the terms old and new guard. Some consider me "old guard" but I think I'm too young and too recently in the scene to be in that category. My more than twenty years of rough sex is too short a period of time to make me much more than a newbie. I still have lots to learn.

Terms are best defined in a dictionary and until we learn what the dictionary says about them, we probably ought not to use them. Instead I would offer alternative terms that are less clouded in meaning and really point to the differences in attitudes that we find in our midst: conservator and innovator.

As I discuss the above, please keep in mind that the operative word here is attitude, "a mental position with regard to a fact or state; feeling or emotion toward a fact or state." One's attitude influences one's actions; hence what one feels about a certain thing will dictate how one will act or react to it.

For instance, I don't generally put a whole lot of stock in class distinction when it comes to how I treat people. I tend to judge them by their actions, not their looks, their net worth, or their educational credentials. That said, I am not always very successful in doing so. When a purple-haired young man comes into my class wearing outlandish attire, I have to remind myself that I'm there to teach, not critique costume.

Like most people, I'm not consistent, either. Whereas I say that I'm a "low protocol kind of guy" I admire strict adherence to good choreography and keeping to the script at lodge meetings. (We Masons call it "ritual" and "floor work.") My slaves don't have many protocols but the few they have I love to see and enforce.

I invite my readers to visit http://www.iron-rose.com/IR/docs/old_guard.htm on the World Wide Web where they will find a posting of Joseph Bean's excellent article, "Old Guard? If You Say So."

The Old Guard/New Nuard question, then, begins with an

analysis of attitude, which I suggest is often the difference between conservator and innovator. One wants to conserve and preserve the status quo, while the other wants to effect change and improvement. There we see the heart of the question. If you are satisfied with the way things are, then you want to keep them the way they are. If you think you have a better way of doing it, then you'll probably want to implement those "new-fangled ideas."

Hence we have those who hearken back "to the good old days" while others rush forward to make things "better." It is very much a problem of methodology. How should we act to attain our best scene, best relationship, or best lifestyle? Will strict interpretation and high standards improve our lot, or ought we lower standards and show increased tolerance for deviation from that which we currently do?

For us kinky folk, the question is immeasurably complicated by incorrect information. The term "old guard" implies that a group actually exists that acts as an entity that is "guarding" something. This group has elevated status because we call it old and therefore see it as having historical precedence. This is muddled by our tendency to romanticize the past as the "good old days."

I often think of the 1950's as the good old days. Why not? I was not yet a teenager and was unaware of any of the struggles that my parents faced. I lived ignorant of mortgage payments, doctor bills, work schedules, and home repairs. I didn't have to pay bills, decide menus, do laundry, or negotiate much more than whether we would play cops and robbers or cowboys and Indians.

Much of that erroneous information about the old guard comes from reading fiction compounded by an acute lack of original records and testimonies. The Leather Archives and Museum is attempting to remedy this situation, but it is a long and arduous task.

In fact there were many people whom we would now consider old guard and each of them was as different as their ages, genders, orientations, and locations would indicate. Leathermen on the east coast had different standards than those on the west. Heterosexual urban practitioners lived a different lifestyle than the renegade Gay bikers who had rough sex in the woods.

Nor were groups homogeneous. When I walked into Jewels in New Orleans in the early 80's I saw men dressed in formal head-to-toe black leather standing next to guys in torn jeans and dirty boots. Some were into protocols, other just wanted to get laid. There was just as much variety then as now. At one time I asked Chuck Renslow (who entered our BDSM community in 1948) about it and he remarked that at the original Gold Coast (circa 1960) there were just as many outlandish hangers-on as there seem to be today. Let me keep the record clear, though; those are my words, not his.

The problem is further complicated by the changes we

go through in life. Carl Jung summarizes what he saw as the two great stages of life: youth and maturity: "As a rule, the life of a young person is characterized by a general unfolding and a striving towards concrete ends; his neurosis, if he develops one, can be traced to his hesitation or his shrinking back from this necessity. But the life of an older person is marked by a contraction of forces, by the affirmation of what has been achieved, and the curtailment of further growth. His neurosis comes mainly from his clinging to a youthful attitude which is now out of season. Just as the young neurotic is afraid of life, the other one shrinks back from death."

So in time, the innovators, happy with the changes they have wrought, become the conservators wanting to keep the new status quo, while younger members think they have a better way. In time, every new guard will become, if they live long enough, part of the next old guard.

Yes, I admit it. The flower child of the late 60's, the war protester, the back-to-the-land Jesus Freak that I was, sounds more and more like my traditional, patriarchal father. I never wanted to grow up to be as "old fashioned" as my Dad, but my hearing loss and arthritis sure make me feel like he must have felt when he was nearing 60, and that was nearly 30 years ago.

As my long-gone friend Father Alliot used to say, "The more things change, the more they stay the same."

Another Closet

October 2, 1995

In two different conversations last week, the question was raised as to why I was into SM. In both cases my answer led to our talking about the mystical side of leather.

It's a topic that you can often find in my writing, if you are able to read the subtleties between the lines of technique, experience, and philosophy. Bill's and Joe's questions pulled any hope of subtlety right away. Here are my more apparent thoughts on the subject, ones I often keep in the closet.

As I reflect on the more powerful scenes that I've had, several come to mind very quickly. Each of them held some kind of metaphysical or paranormal, psychic if you will, experience. The first occurred more than ten years ago with Steven, my slave at the time.

We had been playing for an hour or so and I was in a real "take over his body" mood. I had been doing a lot of ass-playing with him and had given him an enema. He was sitting on the stool as I fondled his genitals. It was a heavy duty moment that only two very intimate friends could be expected to share.

The scene had quietly flowed into a high level of intensity. Both of us were "buzzing" with delightful (non-drug induced) sensations. Suddenly we both had an indescribable experience. Something passed between us, engulfed us, lifted us to some celestial plane. It was what I have come to call a "white lightning" experience.

It was pleasant and felt very safe and warm. There was no fear or danger associated with it, but it was mysterious, otherworldly.

When it had passed, I looked Steven in the eye and asked, "Did you feel what I just felt?" Indeed he had. I gently ended the scene. We both cleaned up and went to bed, not untouched by the power that had passed between us.

Scenes with experiences like that one are rare, but they happen. During two other scenes, the bottoms with whom I was playing recounted past life "experiences", that is, while I was dominating them and had each of them well tied up, they "saw" what

143

looked like the two of us living in some past time, doing things with (and to) each other.

In my play with Lynn, I have had the sensation of "seeing" entities in the room: faces of gargoyles and gods, demons, and angels.

The "angel" sightings, for lack of a better term, look like spheres of white light or glowing globes. Sometimes the circle I see turns into an eye. As I am floating in SM-induced ecstasy, I often see a "darkness" filled with pinpoints of light.

The quotation marks I've used in the sentences above illustrate how difficult it is to relate these things. I remember one night when I had Michael tied up to a St Andrews Cross and was whipping him. He seemed to faint and so I very quickly untied him and gently lowered him to the ground. What had happened was that he was approaching one of those rare transcendent moments.

I'm reminded in all this that there are strong resemblances to Native American vision quests, Sufi dancing, even Pentecostal "anointings." There's another word in quotes!

These exceptional moments are just that: rare, unpredictable, unexpected. One of the problems about writing about them is that they are difficult to describe; the other is that I run the risk of making them sound spooky.

The overwhelming sense one has while in these altered states is that of peace. I can't speak for what the others feel, but for me there are strong feelings of floating, an effortless drifting into some other reality, one without harm, without threat, without need.

I've come to the self-realization that I am an explorer searching inner worlds. That's not to say I wouldn't volunteer to ride the Voyager. I would, but since I can't, I investigate what I can. My inner world beckons, as does whatever other worlds are out there.

In responding to that beckoning, though, I am convinced that the search must remain holistic. If my only focus in leather play were mysticism, I would think that I was losing it. My physical, emotional, social, and intellectual needs must be equally well regarded. To run off in one direction, while ignoring other and just as valid sides of one's existence, is both foolish and dangerous.

All that is to say that we need to maintain a certain balance, a healthy skepticism, and a sense of humor. Yes, spiritualism is a part of SM, but so are emotional release, fraternity, excitement, and pleasure. Throw in practicality, reason, curiosity, love, and lust as well. SM is as multi-faceted as any human endeavor can be. We need to keep a variety of aspects in mind as we play.

Head in the clouds, feet on the earth, heart in love, mind in reason, emotions free. The trick is to let all parts of ourselves run free without allowing any one side to dominate the action. Let

loose emotionally, so to speak, but let your mind notice what is happening and let your body respond accordingly. Of course, all this brings more questions to mind than answers. Take, for instance, the play that Mike and I had this past weekend.

For starters, since Mike and I are lovers of more than two years, we are comfortable and trusting with each other. Our play always comes easily and naturally. We know each other intimately, to say the least, and so it is easy to let go with each other. Nothing holds us back.

As our play progressed, we were hot to trot. Porno movies stimulated our sight. The bed was wide and comfortable, the lights dim. I had given Michael a good spanking. Throughout the night he had used every part of his body to arouse me, to give me pleasure. There had been all the usual sucking, kissing, petting (now there's an old word from high school!), fingering, etc. Passion was running high.

I put on a condom, lubricated Michael's ass, and began to fuck him furiously. I did my best to shove my cock as deeply as possible as I climbed up his back and kissed his neck. I rubbed my pubic hairs into the crack of his ass, pushing bones against bones. It was great

As this was happening I felt "the animal" in me letting loose. Now this is hard to put into words. I can't tell you what happened, but I can tell you what I felt. You'll have to come to your own conclusions as to whether I'm deluded, crazy, mystical, or just imagining it all. I can't tell you if it happened or not, but I can state that it affected me as if it happened, so what difference does it make?

And what is "it"? I felt myself becoming another entity, or so I think. Or maybe I felt another entity taking me over, or riding Michael with me. Or maybe I am more than one self and at this moment, the animal, gargoyle, wolf, demon-part of me let loose. I honestly don't know. In any case, I began growling. I bit his neck and clawed at his chest, my arms holding him tightly.

I know that something was happening. It was as if we had passed from Mike's bedroom through a door into some other space and time. After a moment or so, the passion passed. As I withdrew my cock, I found myself lying next to my lover, content and curious. I felt deeply in love with Michael.

I'm ready for more. Let's explore. Who knows what lies at the moment of our next orgasm?

Levels of Intensity

June 9, 2005

When I began exploring the joys of fetish I would have never imagined what the ensuing years would bring. For the record I flagged gray left, which meant that I was a top into mild S&M. This weekend's play certainly shows I've changed in ways that would have scared the shit out of me in 1983.

For the curious and the neophytes reading this essay, let me add two remarks. First off, flagging left means I wore a gray handkerchief in my back left pocket, one of many ways to signal my proclivities. More importantly, let me assure you that involvement in edgier, more drastic, or more difficult SM practices usually comes only slowly over a long period of time and for many never comes at all. In this subculture you are the arbiter of what you will and will not do and when and with whom you will do it.

Progression in intensity is, and ought to be, based on experience. In scuba diving we begin with the easy stuff in the classroom, proceed to the shallow end of the swimming pool, move then to dives of less than twenty feet, and only after practice and experience under the watchful eyes of a certified instructor do we move to dives of 40, 60, and eventually, 90 feet. So, too, should our kink follow an easy and guided progression.

It is the same for many other processes as well. We begin riding a bike under an adult's supervision on a bike with training wheels. I trust you get my point. To proceed otherwise is to act foolishly and to take unadvisable risks.

What it is that we do falls into the same category. We learn our kink progressively, and no one should try to plunge in over their heads. At all times it is important to know one's comfort level and play at that level until one has the desire, confidence, and experience necessary to venture further. It is in this process that trust becomes all-important. One must trust both oneself and one's partner in order to make the progression both wise and attainable.

Easy floggings with soft deerskin implements become harsher over time as more power and stingier whips are used. In time the whipping may progress to heavy flogging and then when the proper circumstances are present you might negotiate a bloodless scene with a single tail. Successful negotiation and experience here may lead to a full-fledged whipping that leaves your back bloody and your soul soaring -- but that ought never to be a quick move from novice to expert.

Ski slopes are marked with levels of difficulty for a reason. Those same reasons apply to a good number of the fetishes that we might enjoy.

This is not to dissuade a novice-to-leather reader from playing with more experienced players. In fact I urge you to do just that. Although two neophytes can often, as I did in those good old days, have fun with each other, there is a great deal more to be learned from players who are more advanced than oneself.

I seldom fail to shake my head when newcomers tell me they avoid seasoned kinksters. As a matter of fact it is just that kind of player with whom it is safest to play, as they have the experience necessary to best guide the novice, give proper instruction and, most importantly, accurately read their partner's body language to quickly discern and avoid problems. Contrary to many novices' expectations, the seasoned player is quite often very willing to play with them, as there are real satisfactions in both teaching new folk and watching them advance.

Advancing in SM is a matter of peaks, valleys, and plateaus. In the course of time it is the peak experiences that keep us coming back for more. That "more" is not just more of the same but rather a "more" that will drive us up higher peaks.

The problem with that approach (if I can call it a problem) is that peaks are not easily re-created. There is seldom a formula which one can use to repeat a peak, as the variables in attaining bliss are myriad and difficult to properly align. Remember that not every experience will be a peak experience.

Less forgettable, of course, is the knowledge that some experiences are downers. I have yet to find a way to escape the occasional valley when it comes to sex, the night when things just don't go right or as well as one might have fantasized or negotiated. It would be non-productive for me to write that one ought not to be bothered by such a fate, because bothered we will be.

On the more positive side I dare say that your bummers, failures, and less-than-pleasant scenes will actually be better learning experiences than those sought-after peak experiences. That's no reason to seek bad experiences, but they do show that there is a silver lining in every cloud.

The trick here is to look at what one can learn when one fucks up. Rather than assume the victim role when shit happens in the dungeon, we need to take responsibility for our part in the scene's co-creation and use the lessons therein to modify our techniques, our communications, and our negotiations.

Herein we must maintain a critical balance. Too many "no's" and we'll never progress. Too few "no's" and we're in over our heads in situations that will only lead to greater disappointment.

The needed balance is found within yourself and your ability and willingness to trust your partner. Discuss with him or her exactly how you feel. Let him or her know your limits, your hopes, and your fears. Full and honest communication is the key to successful negotiations, which are the springboard to more peaks and fewer failings.

For the more experienced players among us, the problem of intensity is different as it raises the serious question of how intense, how high a peak is possible if we are to remain safe, sane, and legal. Mutilation, to use an extreme example, may be the ultimate sadistic trip but it will probably put one at the wrong end of a jail sentence. We therefore may need to find ways to increase intensity without increasing the possibility of injury or harm.

Since control is one of my many fetishes, I have found that control of my slavish partner has limits. After all, Patrick has to go to work on most mornings and we both have mundane, out-of-the-dungeon lives to live in order to support our play. Rather than exercise more control over one man, then, I have chosen to exercise control over more men. Therein my intensity is increased without the necessity of there being too much control experienced by one man.

Of course that means that Patrick does experience greater control from me, but it is of the type that interferes less in the real world. He has, for instance, to submit to the fact that I am playing with Matt rather than him — though, to be honest, the time often comes in the evening, if possible, that I control both of them in the dungeon at the same time. Voila, my play is more intense for me but not necessarily more intense for them. Thus the path to intensity is a fact of what we do. Enjoy your navigation there.

The Intermediate Zone

December 21, 2006

Eastern mystics write about a state on the road to enlightenment called The Intermediate Zone. In rather simplified form it's a state of mind between an un-awakened consciousness, i.e., one that has a "normal" view of reality, and that of the enlightened mind, which I will let you define for yourself.

The zone is a lot like the mindset of one who is caught in their own vision of reality, one filled with the hubris of their own self-worth, one who is so fixated on some doctrine, belief, or self-centered perception that they become "So heavenly-minded they are no earthly good." Other words apply as well, such as "delusional," "egotistical," even "psychotic," though more often than not we find it manifest in much less drastic terms such as "filled with self-importance," "full of him/herself," "selfish," "rude," or "arrogant." It can also be a state of confusion, doubt, or fear.

In Leather terms it is the hubris of the self-appointed Master who has forgotten that his own shit has a smell to it, whose testosterone-filled ego blinds him to kindness, respect of others, and humility. The same can be said of bottoms who are so self-deprecating that they have lost all self-respect. You don't, after all, have to be an Indian guru to get caught in The Intermediate Zone.

But there is more to this zone than just testosterone, as a wide variety of influences throw us into that zone, affecting our perception and our judgment. Some of these are out of our control, such as illness, the side effects of medication, depression, and injury. Other influences sweep us off our feet, such as alcohol, recreational drugs, excitement, hysteria, and, yes, endorphin rushes and great scenes. Fantasies of all sorts may distort our rationality. I am amazed, for instance, at the reactions of people who are so desperately looking for a scene or a relationship that they throw caution to the wind.

The cure for all of this is balance, that fine point between rationality and emotive responses, order and chaos, rigidity and fluidity, to name just a few of the poles that affect human behavior. The ancient Greeks ascribed the two forces to two sons of

149

Zeus: Apollo, the beautiful, manly, and orderly god, patron of the well-built, well-run city and its rule of law; and Dionysius, aka Bacchus in the Roman pantheon, the god of wine, orgy, chaos and the underworld, a cross-dressing reveler in the countryside, man in feminine attire, half-god, half-human.

It is well-known that Apollo was consulted by the priests at Delphi, the ancient world's most renowned temple. What is less-well known is that his half brother Dionysius was consulted there as well, Apollo during one half of the year, Dionysius the other. It was the Greek way of finding balance, understanding as they did that the better way was in the middle, neither strictly ruled by reason nor erratically driven by passion.

Jung wrote much about the same archetypes, discussing at length the relationship of the (Apollonian) conscious and the (Dionysian) unconscious. Consciousness is the world of reason, perception, cognition, and volition. The unconscious is unknown, the dark side, emotive, instinctual, and intuitive. In those terms they seem far removed from the world of Leather, yet such is not the case. The Old Guard/New Guard dynamic, to mention only one example, reflects exactly that polarity.

In broader terms much of what we do in the world of BDSM is an attempt to attain what we call bottom space (or top space if you favor that side of life). And what is bottom space in psychological terms? Simply an altered state of consciousness, "those states of consciousness in which the individual feels one or more qualitative (and possibly one or more quantitative) shifts in mental functioning, so that he believes himself to be in an ASC.[1]"

The shift is from the everyday experience of the conscious to that of the unconscious. It is that dream-state of bliss, euphoria, runner's high, floating and drifting, into which we are inducted by scenes that go so very well. A rare event to be sure, but glimpsed often enough that we return time and again seeking its pleasurable experience and its fleeting freedom from the mundane world in which we live.

In less dramatic terms the experience is an everyday occurrence, as when the top finds him or herself loving the control he/she has, or the bottom feels the joy of belonging, of serving, of receiving the attention he or she seeks. And so we are caught in the flow of what our unconscious brings us, loving the fleeting pleasure of the experience (a very good experience at that), and cherishing the more common sense of enjoyment in being part of our kinky culture.

Still we find that Apollo must have his rule in our lives. We seek safe, sane, and consensual experiences: dungeons where we can play without concern; partners that we can trust; relationships that enhance our lives rather than drive us to the madness

1 Tart, Charles T. , Editor, *Altered States of Consciousness*, John Wiley & Sons, Inc., New York, 1969, page 2.

of Dionysius. We need rules for good order, a structure that will hold, sustain, and support the action that leads to the freedom of ecstasy. The architect's orderly arrangement of building materials affords us a safe place in which to revel freely. The dungeon master's observant care of the players preserves health and mutual comfort.

Yet it is just as true that "The letter of the law kills, the spirit gives life." The dogmatism of the lawmaker will crush creativity, destroy intimacy, reduce a scene to a sterile, lifeless skeleton of its real nature. In protecting the entity, be it scene, place, relationship, or organization, the PC police will drive out all semblance and presence of the emotional, the mystical, and the divine. Our techniques will become assembly-line ghosts of their real purpose. What is meant to be art, descends to craft and from craft becomes mere machinations, cold, unfeeling actions of rote without heart and soul.

How then do we judge? What might be our criteria? It is discernment "to detect with other senses than vision." As the Scriptures note: "By their fruits you will know them." What is the effect of your rational rule or your strong feeling? Is it peace, harmony, and joy? Do your actions engender trust, honor and respect? The goal here is harmony, the "pleasing or congruent arrangement of parts; correspondence, accord; internal calm: tranquility."

Jung continues his explanation with the idea that we strive to arrive at individuation, the harmonious balance of both the conscious and the unconscious, the integration of both aspects of our psyche into our lives, becoming ever more the fully human person. Lofty sentiments to be sure, but I believe that what it is that we do affords us just that possibility.

When Rivers Merge

June 17, 2001

In 2001, I had the pleasure of attending the South East Leather Fest (S.E.L.F.) in Atlanta. Their very full program offered something kinky for nearly everyone and I had a good time watching that "something." My weekend there gave me a great deal of food for thought. Allow me to share some of those musings.

First off, I went as an attendee. I did so for several reasons, not the least of which was so I could see a couple of hot guys who had invited me to stay with them. They were gracious hosts, chauffeurs, and eye-candy. Thanks, guys. I also went alone, something I'll probably not do again. My slaves treat me so well that I find cruising too much work. I know you probably think that means I'm lazy, and you're right. You might also call me spoiled.

S.E.L.F. is a three-day event that combines four contests (Mr. SE Drummer, SE Drummerboy, Ms. SE Leather, and International Master and slave), two parties, exhibits, and workshops. As such it offers something kinky across all sorts of lines: gay, lesbian, het, bi, and try-anything. The convergence of Old and New Guard, Pro Domme (Professional Dominatrix), members of motorcycle clubs, play parties and munches, Masters, slaves, Daddies, boys, and Goths made for a real cornucopia of partying.

My New Year's resolution was to "get out more," as I had begun to feel that I was losing touch with the scene because of my stay-at-home habits. Additionally, I am seldom invited to speak at these assemblies, most probably because "out of sight, out of mind." Since no one was promoting my teaching abilities, I decided that I'd better promote myself. Hint, hint.

I was right, of course, as when I picked up my registration badge I was told "Gee, Jack, if we knew you were coming we would have had you give a workshop." Duh. That's what I get for being hard to get. Since I had no obligations, I could attend whatever workshops I wanted to and had plenty of time to sit and watch teh action as well as talk with a number of good friends who were also in attendance.

I was most pleased to hear Viola Johnson share her experiences on slave-training. For further details, I suggest you read her book, *To Love, To Serve, To Obey*, as it documents an important part of our past: Old School slavery of the most genteel and aristocratic sort. This, of course, is one of the rivers I saw merging in Atlanta. Vi's experience as a full-time slave in service to professional Dominatrices (at least that's what they seem to have been) represents a very large segment of our kinky culture, even if we Gay Leathermen have been somewhat oblivious to its existence.

Another river, and one that is flooding us, is the group of heterosexuals who are first meeting on the Internet, then forming "munches" so they can meet in public, an act invariably followed by the formation of a group that plays, teaches, organizes, and grows. Once again we Gays may be somewhat oblivious to this movement, but it promises to be huge.

Then there are what The Eulenspiegel Society (TES) calls TNG -- The Next Generation. To put it mildly there were boys everywhere, and you can define boys any way you like: tops, bottoms, male, female, trans, submissive, and spunky.

Another surprise, the Lesbian contingent, also demonstrated how out of it I can be. Unlike most of the women I know, they were proud to be kinky. Like the boys, they came in all sorts: Masters, slaves, tops, bottoms, switches, butch, femme, petite, and bull.

The exhibit area was a microcosm of this vast convergence. It was certainly more Het than Gay and the exhibitors' wares spanned a wide spectrum as well. The large number of tables featuring single-tails and/or knives gave emphasis to the growing popularity of "blood sports."

Now some of my reactions may have been based on the fact that I was in Atlanta. Even though it is a thoroughly modern city, it is still located in the Deep South and its Leather culture is going to reflect that circumstance. Still I felt that the scene I was witnessing is probably more generally the case America-wide than I am used to. The truth is that clear delineations are quickly fading in the face of the twenty-first century. It's a situation that Leather folk must face, though doing so is not a threat, it's an opportunity.

As we came up to the thirty-second anniversary of Stonewall and the emergence of Gay Lib (does that term date me or what?) we saw the rapid disappearance of stereotypes among those who are following us in kink. To many of those under the age of thirty, there is no need to be Gay, Lesbian, Bisexual or Heterosexual: they are simply themselves and sexual orientation poses little of

153

concern to them. Indeed, there was a time or two during the weekend when I honestly could not discern a person's gender. In fact, in at least two situations I had to lean over to a friend and whisper "Is he a he or a she?" The play parties, though I didn't go to any of them, reflected this trend as well, as they were held in pansexual play areas that made male-only spaces look like an anachronism. Times are changing.

The problem, of course, is that when I was in my early twenties we knew enough not to trust anyone over thirty. Thirty years later, I am in that category and occasionally feel like I'm being left out. Well, the truth may be that I tend to leave myself out.

Most of the workshops that I attended were on the topic of Master and slave relationships. Since this is one of my interests, it gave me the most food for thought. Sitting in the audience I was able to hear others' perspectives and see how other men and women structured their D/s lives. Frankly, it all made me feel somewhat extreme.

My New England influences, my rather classical education, my immersion in Philosophy, and my years as a writer have brought me thus far. As I listened to Masters Taino, Steve Sampson, and Dean Waldradt, I began feeling very conservative. Now my life isn't theirs and the reciprocal is true as well. Each of us has fashioned unique relationships under the guise of Master/slave. One aims for a more familial setting; another is more permissive with his boys; another has more protocols and non-traditional pairings. In it, there is a real sense that it works for them, which is most likely the most important of conclusions.

Our individual styles may vary but we still have a lot to learn from one another. Vi's sharing, for instance, that in her youth, "slaves taught the slaves," was an insight that I hadn't heard before, since in Gay circles, Masters most often teach their boys/slaves themselves.

I don't have a crystal ball capable of telling me where these rivers run once they run together, but I can sense that it is an unstoppable flood. The mixing of genders, or orientations, of kinks, and of lifestyles will produce a new sub-culture, diverse, mellow, tolerant, and accommodating. There will be, as never before, something for everyone, and I mean everyone.

Altered Spaces

Subspace

There are many names for the mind trip that we in the subculture of BDSM most often call "subspace." We also call it an "out of body experience," "going deep," and "topspace." Whatever name you give it, it is an often-sought but rarely achieved "trip" of extraordinary bliss, joy, and peace. In scholarly literature it is called an Altered State of Consciousness (ASC).

As recounted in my book *Philosophy in the Dungeon*, the first time it happened to me was in church at about the age of twelve, during the reception of Holy Communion. I also described a similar event I had in 1985 (age 39) during a very kinky scene in which I was anally dominating my slave/partner. Though both events are difficult to describe, they included an overwhelming sense of peace, the feeling of being surrounded by a beautiful white light, and a strong awareness of the presence of God.

The most common element of this experience is the easiest to describe; that is, whatever happens is difficult to describe. "Ineffable" is the academic word for "incapable of being expressed." Though I wrote "difficult to describe" I might as well have written "impossible to describe" and would have been just as accurate. Whatever the experience is, it seems to be some kind of awareness of one's Inner Self, an Inner Voice, the experience of one's Soul, Essence, or Life Force, whether such a phenomenon is personal or not.

In spite of this descriptive difficulty, some literature attempts a description. One appears in *Altered States of Consciousness*, edited by Charles T. Tart: "Altered States of Consciousness are those states of consciousness in which the individual feels one or more qualitative (and possibly one or more quantitative) shifts in mental functioning, so that he believes himself to be in an ASC."

I don't find this to be a very satisfying definition, as it relies on highly subjective criteria to determine whether one is in such a state. Simply put, Tart is saying, "If you think you're in altered state then you are." On the other hand, how can we define it except subjectively? There are, after all, occurrences of altered states that an external observer might have no way of knowing when they are happening to someone else.

Before I proceed with this discussion, I would like to make two observations. The first is that a full-blown BDSM-related ASC is a rare experience. Intense, overwhelming, and deeply profound ASCs don't happen very often. They are not easily attained, nor easily replicated. Secondly, mild ASCs — those that give glimpses, bits and "tastes" of more profound experiences — are much more prevalent.

In spite of their rarity, ASCs occur often enough that we can describe the general characteristics that Tart calls "Signs of an altered state." He lists them as follows. The explanations of the characteristics are mine:

• Alterations in thinking. In an ASC, we think differently, having for the time being an alteration in how we think about a given topic. This may include a better understanding or a new insight, though such an alteration may not be enduring.

• Disturbed time sense. There is a perception that the normal progression of time has shifted. This may mean that it seems that time moves very slowly or that it passes more quickly. A good example of this phenomenon (some people say) often occurs when smoking marijuana, when time seems to move very slowly. Seconds, for instance, may appear to take minutes to pass.

• Loss of control. The person experiencing an ASC often feels as if they are floating or drifting freely in a universe without gravity, that they are loose, free of all restraint and the ability to direct any action at all. Although one feels powerless, this is rarely a frightening experience. Instead the loss of control is experienced as a liberation from the need to control, that we are being cared for by some superior power or have moved into some safe, secure universe that is void of harm.

• Change in emotional expression. Simply put, we feel differently when we are in an ASC and so we show that difference emotionally, such as with laughter, crying, or quietude.

• Body image change. Here we perceive our bodies as different, perhaps stronger, more beautiful, or less faulty. This might be accompanied by a different self-image or a(n erroneous) sense of immortality or infallibility.

• Perceptual distortions. Colors may appear more intense; objects larger or magnified, our sight able to see at microscopic levels. We may experience music, visions, auras, and other psychic phenomena.

• Change in meaning or significance. We appreciate altered meanings and things make sense in a different (but not necessarily correct) way than when we are in normal consciousness.

• Sense of the ineffable. As I wrote above, an ASC is often un-describable and leaves the one experiencing it speechless.

• Feelings of rejuvenation. Similar to the body image change, we perceive ourselves as healthier, rejuvenated, enlivened and empowered.

•   Hypersuggestibility. Those who are experiencing an ASC may become more easily influenced by their own ideas or the directions of others who may be guiding or facilitating the experience.

My friend Robert, in reviewing an earlier version of this chapter, noted that "Tate's characterizations sound like a trip on LSD." He's right, of course, as you might have suspected if you took the time to read the footnote. His book was published in 1969.

The important point is not the source or causation of the experience but rather that all ASCs have certain characteristics in common. That doesn't mean that all ASCs have all the characteristics, but that all have some. This basic similarity leads to the conclusion that a runner's high and a drug-induced high are similar, as are the visions and prophesies of a Pentecostal woman in a trance state and the psychic experiences of a bottom being flogged while tied to a St. Andrews Cross.

The use of drugs to induce an altered state of consciousness poses problems for those of us seeking legal, psychologically sound, and safe means of exploring our inner selves. Though there are recognizable similarities in the ASCs, there are also profound differences that must be taken into consideration. In any case, I am not advocating the use of drugs but rather the natural pathways that we have to access the depths of our own psyches.

What we are left with when we try to describe and define an ASC is a loss of words. By definition that makes sense, since if indeed it is a journey into the unknowable, then how can we presume to know it?

I am not offering these essays to dissect ASCs. They are what they are and, quite frankly, ought simply to be enjoyed. If we can eventually arrive at some understanding of what causes them, how they happen, what they affect and what they mean, then all the better. Lacking that, though, might I suggest that we simply enjoy them? After all, healthy BDSM is meant to be fun. If it lacks that necessary component, then we ought to abandon it for those pastimes that are enjoyable.

The Psyche according to Jung

It's more than presumptuous for me to be writing an essay on Jungian Psychology, as I can hardly do justice to Dr. Jung's teachings in one short chapter. That said, I'll do my best, and strongly advise you to read Dr. Jung's works yourself, thereby coming to your own conclusions.

Jung was a medical doctor who studied Psychology, which was then a fairly new area of Science, under Sigmund Freud, in the late 1800's and early 1900's. In time his views deviated from those of Freud and he developed his own theses, now generally called Jungian Psychology. His studies and writings delved deeply into the structure of Mind and reflect years of experience as a counselor and therapist. Philosophical enquiry, significant research in mythology and ancient and primitive societies, and the meaning of ritual were all subjects that he studied in formulating his hypotheses.

In time he understood the Human Mind as a composite of the Conscious and the Unconscious, each "part" having a primary focus: Ego being the "center" of Consciousness; Self that of the Unconscious. He wisely noted that such a distinction could only be made in order to understand Mind. It was only an allegory, not a clear illustration of what Mind actually might be. As the slow gradations in the accompanying illustration on page 161 show, there are no clear delineations between Ego and Consciousness or Self and the Unconscious. Indeed there is only the whole and a continuum from one aspect of Mind to another.

What we can ascribe to each part are various functions of mind. In Jung's schematic, the Conscious controls the realms of cognition, perception, memory, reason, and volition, while the Unconscious deals with instinct, emotion, intuition, dream states, and the automatic physical functions.

Conscious knowledge begins with perception, as data enters our minds through the five senses, becoming neurological information translated by our brains into perception. Most of those sensations are simply shunted away as our brains selectively process sensed reality to thought, feelings, and memory. Memory resides in our consciousness as that which can be recalled, though there is certainly a great deal of "forgotten memory" in the subconscious and unconscious areas of our minds. Our minds abstract information into knowledge and eventually into wisdom.

As we mature from childhood to adulthood, we develop our ability to reason and thence to make decisions (volition). Each of these processes involves choice; hence they are found in our consciousness.

Involuntary processes of the mind involve those activities which we do instinctively, such as nurse as babies, and automatic physical functions such as regulation of our heartbeat. Some of these automatic processes, such as breathing, can also be controlled by the conscious self. Emotions arise naturally and spontaneously from unconscious responses to stimuli, though what we choose to do with emotional states can be directed by the conscious self. Intuition, like dream states, also arises from the unconscious.

The above consideration of knowledge through sensation can be challenged by intuitive knowledge which enters our awareness without the use of the five senses. This is information that comes from the subconscious (information that at one time

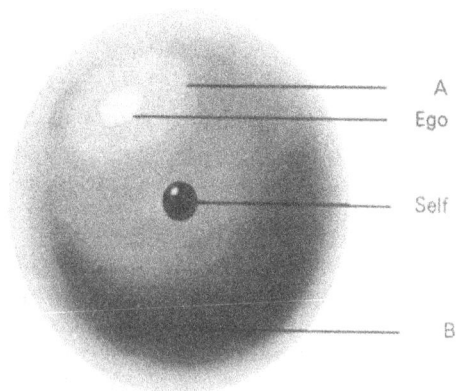

Illustration is taken from Man and His Symbols.[1] A
refers to the conscious, B to the unconscious.

was conscious and now is not) or from the unconscious, though
some would say that even that information had to come to us
originally via our senses. Others posit that the information comes
from extra-sensory perception, commonly called ESP. So, while
we acknowledge the place of the unconscious in knowledge, we
generally consider it "extra" and in some ways unreliable.

Jung's theory developed the idea that information in our
Unconscious was Collective Memory, being passed on in the species from primeval and inherited memories and what he calls
Archetypes, patterns and concepts that reflect universal ideas,
such as the archetype of Mother or Warrior.

We often think of ourselves as that which is more properly
called the Ego. Jung sees a difference between the Ego and the
Self, the first being as much a product of environment and social-
ization, the second being more closely reflective of the authentic
person.

The Unconscious (since we are unconscious of it) remains the area of the unknown; hence it is referred to as the Dark
Side of the personality. Though that nomenclature is loaded with
connotations of evil, it simply refers to the fact that that which is
unconscious is unknown, until through various processes it is
brought into our conscious awareness.

Awareness is the basis of altered states, since what is
altered is awareness itself, as we become aware of that which
was hidden in our unconscious or, to put it another way, we lose

1 Jung, Carl G. *Man and His Symbols*, Doubleday & Company Inc. Garden City, New York, 1969, page 161. **161**

awareness of our usual conscious perspective.

The Psychological basis for an ASC is that some catalyst moves our awareness out of its ordinary state into an altered one. In our subculture, BDSM-related activity is that catalyst, as pain, bondage, sensory overload or deprivation, role-playing, or suggestion cause this shift.

The shift in awareness may occur for any of several reasons, or several reasons combined. It may, for instance, be the result of the release of endorphins or pain-blocking hormones into the blood stream; it may be induced by hypnotic suggestion, or by a meditative state encouraged by the immobility of bondage.

The Meaning of the Experience

In trying to understand the meaning, implications, and value of ASCs, it is important that we not lose sight of their being simply pleasurable. An essay such as this runs the serious risk of taking an event which has fun, relaxation, enjoyment, bonding, stress reduction, and play as its purposes and relegating it to some kind of scientific experiment, cut up into shreds that lose their intrinsic value and purpose.

Still there may be something to be gained by attempting to understand the world of the unconscious as discovered in an ASC, since by doing so we may gain some understanding of reality in general and of ourselves in particular. As William James noted in 1929:

> Our normal waking consciousness...is but one special type of consciousness, whilst all about it, parted from it by the filmiest of screens, there lie potential forms of conscious entirely different. We may go through life without suspecting their existence; but apply the requisite stimulus, and at a touch they are all there in all their completeness, definite types of mentality which probably somewhere have their field of application and adaptation. No account of the universe in its totality can be final which leaves these other forms of consciousness quite disregarded. How to regard them is the question -- for they are so discontinuous with ordinary consciousness. Yet they may determine attitudes though they cannot furnish formulas, and open a region though they fail to give a map. At any rate, they forbid a premature closing of our accounts with reality.[1]

Altered States of Consciousness lead us to experience that there is more to human existence than meets the eye, or any of the other senses. What it is that we "meet" remains darkly hid-

1 James, William, 1929, pages 378-379, as quoted in *Altered States of Consciousness*, edited by Charles T. Tart, Jon Wiley & Sons, Inc., 1969, page 21.

den but beckons nevertheless, tempting us with an expanded view, partial though it may be, of reality.

It is important to note that whatever view an ASC offers us is incomplete, merely a glimpse into another state of consciousness. Not only is our perception of this state incomplete, it is difficult to comprehend because it lacks the "logic" of our normal perception. Hence we often see dreams, for example, as disjointed and unreasonable, the action proceeding in a non-linear fashion, scenes in the dream appearing unrelated, the players as composites of people we seem to remember, or, when familiar, we find them in roles or situations completely alien to our normal knowledge of them.

Nevertheless, my experience with altered states is that they provide me with experiences that enhance my mundane life in several ways, including my creativity, my sense of balance and harmony, my perception of my "place" in the universe, and a greater awareness of my full human potential.

Increased sense of belonging/relationship to Universe

The most profound and lasting effect of an ASC is that it impresses me with the feeling of belonging. As I've written, an ASC is often accompanied by a sense of well-being, of peace, of being part of the greater universe. It is a distinct feeling of unity, of connectedness to all that is. I sense that I am an important part of a greater whole, no longer cut off or alienated but rather "where I belong."

Though there is certainly a sense of something "outside" of me when it happens, there is also a strong feeling that that something is within me as well, that the Universe is, in some inexplicable way, contained within me. This experience has come to me during BDSM-induced ASCs as well as during more profound times of meditating.

That feeling naturally leads to a feeling of balance and harmony. It is exactly that feeling that one can take from an ASC and apply in one's usual state of consciousness. If nothing else, this is the value of an ASC.

Creativity

In my own situation, the experience of an ASC, whether full blown or partial, has been an increase in my creative abilities. Images and ideas realized in an ASC have provided the basis for much of my literary work in recent years. At times it is simply the ability to refresh myself with that sense of balance and harmony that has allowed me to return to work refreshed and ready to write. At other times, I have received inspiration while in an ASC and have then been able to bring those ideas back to my work.

I should note that most of these experiences, though similar to BDSM-related experiences, occurred while meditating or in the early waking moments of dreaming. What I have found is an increased integration of my unconscious Self with my conscious Ego, a feeling that I can move, and sometimes am moving, in both realities simultaneously.

ESP

Intuition, Synchronicity, and Manifestation, as aspects of Extra-Sensory Perception, seem to increase as one accustoms oneself to the ASC experience. What may in reality happen is that what has changed is not reality itself but how we perceive it. What becomes permanently shifted, so to speak, is our awareness of life and the way it works. Having experienced altered reality, we come to the conclusion that reality can be altered, and then more easily see it being altered before our very eyes.

Again, none of this is anything upon which we can build solid, defensible conclusions in a materialistic and scientific way. Rather these are pathways to explore as we attempt in some small way to attain our fullest human potential, even as we have yet to fully realize what that might be.

Pathways to an Altered State

One of the important things about altered states is that some of them are so common that we often fail to recognize them as anything out of the ordinary. The best example of this is the fact of sleep, a state in which our usual consciousness ceases and we become unconscious of our surroundings. In this "altered state" we often experience our unconscious in the form of dreams.

The reality of sleep and dreaming is a good context in which to consider altered states. In fact they are out of the ordinary only because we accept our usual state of consciousness as so completely normative, even when we may spend anywhere from six to nine hours a day sleeping and therefore out of our "normal" state of consciousness.

As mentioned in the last chapter, there are many characteristics of an ASC that we can experience as part of our everyday lives. Acts that induce an ASC are myriad: Drugs, Sleep, Music, Meditation, Beauty, Dance, Ritual, Religious Experience, Sensory Deprivation, and Fetish being only the ones that most quickly come to mind. Although one pathway may be sufficient to induce an ASC, it is probable that a multi-path experience is more likely to bring the ASC "aspirant" into such a state.

For example, Religious Experience is usually a combination of beautiful music, quiet meditation or reflection, held in an architecturally beautiful room where ritual is being conducted. Is

164

it any wonder, then, that an ASC induced by BDSM activity ought not also to have multiple factors associated with it?

Encouraging ASCs

How do we enhance a scene to make it more conducive to our experiencing an ASC? Assuming a willingness to go on such a trip, here are some examples of ways to accomplish that. Please note that they cannot replace experience, trust, and the willingness to surrender to the moment. In fact these three conditions are probably absolutely necessary for an ASC to occur.

I will admit that newbies (i.e., people without experience) may at times enter an altered state of consciousness (ASC), but in general practice it takes a fairly good amount of experience before we are able to trust and surrender deeply enough with our partner to have it occur. Experience, first, is necessary as the foundation upon which we can have trust. Trust is necessary if we are going to be able to surrender sufficiently to allow our conscious self to "turn off" as we move into the realm of the unconscious.

In studying ways to encourage entry into an ASC, I have come up with six methodologies for increasing the quality of this intimate experience: Music, Visualization, Breath Work, Meditation, Erotic Touch, and Energetic Control. Each of these could be a book in and of itself, but allow me to at least point you in the right direction and give you some things to think about. Remember, too, that this list is only meant to point you in the right direction and is not all-inclusive by any means.

Before I discuss, I would like to emphasize that none of these techniques are going to replace trust and surrender, nor are they substitutes for good BDSM skills, and safe, sane, and consensual play. On the other hand, you will notice that the list includes none of the usual kinky things that we do. Instead I have tried to look outside of BDSM activity in order to find additional techniques that will encourage the attainment of our SM goals.

You see, there are many ways to attain an ASC and most of them have nothing to do with WIITWD. Adding these non-kinky practices to our dungeon play both increases the intensity of our play and the likelihood of attaining an ASC. Still the fact remains that ASCs are hard to attain, rare in their occurrence, and almost impossible to re-create.

We go to the symphony, to rock concerts, and to discos because music often puts us into an ASC. It is as simple as that. We should be aware of what sounds are in the air when we engage in BDSM as they can dramatically affect our mood, our tempos, and our sensations. Do you want it slow and cuddly or energetic and upbeat? Are you going to flog and whip or mummify and fly?

If you compare the sounds in the room to what you are doing, you will find that they have a great influence on the quality of your play. In fact the DJ in the dungeon is a very important person. The best tops know this and make sure that they are their own DJs or that the DJ is as good at directing the scene as they are, since music has a big part to play in carrying the players where they are going.

I cannot tell you what kind of music to play. You must decide what works for you. Here is my list to give you some music for thought: "Pachabel Canon" by the Academy of Ancient Music, "Spiritlands" by John Huling, "Chant" by the Benedictine Monks of Santo Domingo de Silos, "Tantric Harmonics" by the Gyume Tibetan Monks, "Space-Taculars" by John Williams and The Boston Pops, "Drum Medicine" by David and Steve Gordon, and "Sensual Classics" from BMG Direct Marketing. I also enjoy Horowitz, Beethoven, and Mozart. Notice how eclectic my list is: Classical, Native American, Gregorian, Buddhist, and New Age. A sound for every one of my tastes. Your challenge is to find a sound for every one of yours.

Consider the types of music you enjoy and what kinds of effects they have on you. Experiment in the bedroom and the dungeon to see how various musical styles enhance your pleasure and your experience.

Visualization is a method of imagining a process or an event in such a way that you psychologically experience it. Popularized by author Shakti Gawain in her book, *Creative Visualization*, it would be difficult to describe the process in a few short paragraphs. Instead, let me give a few examples.

I visualize the flow of energy up from the ground, through my legs and torso, then to my arms to my flogger, onto my bottom's back, and returning to the earth. In another scenario I might imagine love projecting out of my heart in the form of light to the heart of my slave. Likewise the light may go from heart to heart and return. We can imagine energy flowing from our hand to the hand of another, or from the Earth up our bodies to the top of our heads, continuing to the sky and then returning as a shower on us.

These visualizations may also be directed by speech, as I suggest to my partner that he or she visualize the same thing that I visualize. It need not be as direct as that sounds, as I may say something that implies the action, such as "Feel the power of the earth surge through my cock into your ass."

Another helpful way to connect is by breathing together, either by alternately sharing breath (I breathe out as you breathe in) or by breathing synchronously, that is we both breathe in and out at the same time. See the essay called "A Primary Technique" on page 45 for more information on this topic.

If you know any meditation techniques (some of which are actually included above) then you might find it helpful to use them, especially when you are bottoming. Meditation itself can put you into an ASC, so it can be easily used to reinforce subspace, while we simultaneously use SM to the same end.

Using muscle relaxation techniques (one way to meditate) is a popular way to dissipate the pain of bottoming and transform it into an ASC. Again, this is a whole topic in itself, so I will advise you to do some of your own research on the subject. Another answer might be that muscle relaxation can be practiced any time and is a valuable exercise in any stressful situation. In short, simply contract a muscle to feel yourself controlling it, then purposefully relax it. With practice you will remember how to relax the muscle group whenever it becomes tense.

This technique is especially helpful during intercourse, when tightening and relaxing anal or vaginal muscles pumps the cock. It is also part of extending or inducing multiple orgasms. Needless to say, the ability to relax muscles also helps to diffuse and mitigate pain, as tense muscles hurt more than relaxed ones.

Another idea has to do with erotic touch. Don't let your sadomasochistic desires overwhelm all the others. The delight of pain, aggressiveness and surrender are all enhanced by tenderness, soothing care, and mutual affection. Mix sweetness with your "sour-ness" and you will magnify the intensity of both. A short gentle stroke after a brutal sting with a whip or a painful slap after a tender kiss both have the same effect -- increasing the depth of the ASC. Frankly I can't emphasize this technique too much and will quickly add, "Don't knock it until you've tried it."

The last idea, though I hope you will search for and find more than this short list offers, is to use Energetic Control. Based on a Tantric understanding of the human body and sexuality, it uses several techniques, such as visualization, breathing, and meditating, in combination to direct the sharing of psychic, physical, and sexual energy between partners.

Too many players (in my not-so-humble opinion) think that a scene is all about BDSM techniques. Neither slaves nor bottoms, neither Masters nor tops live by SM techniques alone. Add a full range of "tools" to your repertoire and a universe of new worlds will open to you, especially the universe within.

What Do We Do with It?

It's all well and good (not to mention imperative) to leave the experience of ASCs in the realm of pure pleasure. But having spent this much time intellectualizing about the subject, we are left with the question of "What do we do with it?"

First and fundamentally, I think it is solely necessary to enjoy the experience. Prodding and stretching it beyond enjoyment will eventually destroy it. That said, perhaps I should stop there, but of course I won't.

The reason I even mention this topic and devote so many pages to it is because it is pleasurable and ASCs hold the potential of having profound, life-changing effects on our lives. That religious experience of Holy Communion certainly contributed to my entering the seminary some eight or ten years later. My Pentecostal experience in 1969 led me to join a Jesus commune two years later, delayed my career for some four years, and put off grad school for some ten years. That white light experience with my slave firmly established me as a strongly committed Leatherman and Master, a lifestyle that has served me well for more than twenty years.

Still the most important long-term effect of my ASC experiences has been a general improvement in the quality of my life. Discovering and being in "contact" with my Inner Self, while certainly challenging to the Ego-based conception of who I was, nevertheless has freed me to live a more authentic and satisfying life.

Jung writes of what he calls "individuation," the coming to wholeness of the human psyche, a harmony arising when the Ego and the Self are in balance. This inner alignment (my words, not his) is the essence of real happiness, contentment, and satisfaction. Without the experience of that inner universe, the outer one (as I see it) will never mean as much or be as beautiful.

This process, as I want to make clear, is greatly subjective and life-long. One does not simply "have an experience" and attain Nirvana. The process we call life may be infused with energy, insight, and direction by time spent in an altered state, but what we do with that state is probably more important than the experience of it.

Without wanting to preach at you, let me suggest seven ways one might find real value in an ASC.

- Find ways to integrate it into your life.
- Explore and seek to know what it is teaching you.
- Discuss its meaning with your partner.
- Open up to it to gain a greater benefit.
- Use it to develop your creativity.
- Allow your life to undergo transformation.
- Understand its application to your way of living.

Having allowed yourself the freedom to learn, to grow, and to change, you too will discover synchronicity, intuitive wisdom, and a fuller manifestation of your potential.

Afterwords

July 2008

There you have it.

In reality, of course, this book can represent only a very small part of "it." There is a great deal more to our kinky lifestyle than can be put to words. Even those pictures that are worth a thousand words can't do jutice to"What it is that we do."

As I reflect on the twenty-five years of changes I have seen this subculture undergo, I am amazed at the great strides we have made: in size, in literature, in knowledge and practice of fetish, in spiritual understanding, in organization, in commerce, and in realizing our potential as sexual explorers.

In 1983 BDSM players were, for the most part, a hidden, underground culture accessible only by diligent search, out-of-sight bars, or discreet reference. There were only four or five books available to the average reader, who would have had a hell of a time trying to finding them. Just counting the hundreds of titles now available, demonstrates what I mean.

To be honest, though, the written word can hardly substitute for active participation in the rich and varied subculture of kinky sex. As I noted in the Preface, *More from the Master* can only point you in a direction. As a book it is all "talk," so to speak. It is up to you to walk the walk.

In that respect I encourage you to find and become involved in one of the thousands of "gateway" groups that welcome the curious, the interested, and yes, the horny into our midst. If you are unsure of how to do this, there are many fine introductory books on the market. Even a simple Internet search will turn up the name of a group where you live.Go to your favorite search engine and type in the name of your city (or a large city near you) and the acronymn BDSM.

One of the major themes in this book is how to deal with fear, since it is fear that keeps one from buying that first book or attending that first meeting. Even we more experienced players know fear as an emotion that affects our lives no matter how much knowledge or experience we have. As much as we learn, there forever remains the unknown. I hope that I have shed at least some light on that "unknown" and that you, too, will seek to learn and grow with us and, having done so, share it with others.

Jack Rinella
Chicago
July, 2008

www.ingramcontent.com/pod-product-compliance
Lightning Source LLC
Chambersburg PA
CBHW052003090426
42741CB00008B/1531